CHRISTMAS JOKES

for Grumpy Blokes

CHRISTMAS JOKES

for Grumpy Blokes

Nick Harris

Michael O'Mara Books Limited

First published in Great Britain in 2020 by
Michael O'Mara Books Limited
9 Lion Yard
Tremadoc Road
London SW4 7NQ

A CIP catalogue record for this book is available from the British Library.

Papers used by Michael O'Mara Books Limited are natural, recyclable
products made from wood grown in sustainable forests. The
manufacturing processes conform to the environmental regulations of
the country of origin.

ISBN: 978-1- 78929-279-4 in paperback print format
ISBN: 978-1-78929-280-0 in ebook format

2 3 4 5 6 7 8 9 10

Illustrations by Andrew Pinder
Designed and typeset by D23
Cover design by Natasha le Coultre

Printed and bound by CPI Group (UK) Ltd, Croydon, CR0 4YY

www.mombooks.com

MIX
Paper from
responsible sources
FSC® C020471
FSC
www.fsc.org

ALWAYS REMEMBER:

*a grumpy bloke is for life,
not just for Christmas . . .*

CONTENTS

INTRODUCTION

Is any time of the year more depressing than Christmas? It's that season of enforced jollity where even the grumpiest of us are required by some imperceptible law to be civil to people whom we have spent the rest of the year trying to avoid, to overeat and drink to the detriment of our health and take part in family games that become so competitive they can start decade-long feuds . . . and all while wearing a coloured paper hat at a jaunty angle.

Those who claim to find Christmas vaguely tolerable point out that it only lasts for a few days, but that's not strictly true. As early as August, when, under normal circumstances, we've only just finished peeling ourselves off Spanish sunbeds, we see the first signs of Yuletide creeping into the shops with reminders that it's only 125 days to Christmas. And those warnings: buy tinsel early because there could be a worldwide shortage this year due to rising sea levels/the economic slowdown/the bogeyman. Take your pick.

By the time we've reached November every trip to a shopping mall means slaloming through a display of inflatable Santas against a backdrop of tinny recordings of Slade, Wizzard or Mariah Carey.

We are lured to these soulless places by the curious obligation we feel to send Christmas cards to people we will probably never see in person again. We have no other contact with them during the year, so on their card we write platitudes like 'Hope you are keeping well' or 'We must meet up again sometime'. The latter can be penned safe in the knowledge that we will not even receive a reply to this suggestion until next year's card. Therefore it will be at least two years down the line before we have to back up our words with actions, and at that point we can revert to 'Hope you are keeping well'.

The run-up to Christmas at work invariably involves the office Christmas lunch, where we pay an exorbitant price for a grey, grizzled slice of turkey that tastes like cardboard, with soggy roast potatoes, vegetables that only cattle would consider tasty and warm white wine. Of course, attendance is compulsory and for the office creep it represents an opportunity to cosy up to the boss. The rest of us sabotage the carefully arranged seating plan so that we can sit next to our friends on the 'naughty table', where any talk of work is strictly banned, and plot when we can safely adjourn to the pub without being missed.

All in all, it is an occasion to be endured rather than enjoyed. And surely there should be a hunting season for carol singers, where at the very least we are allowed to set the dogs on them.

TV advertising strives to ensure that we are never at a loss for ideas of what to buy those dearest to us. Every product – from fungal nail infection cream to a Perry Como CD – is hailed as 'the perfect gift for Christmas'. Why do advertisers think that everyone over the age of sixty automatically yearns for a Perry Como CD when the music of their youth was The Sex Pistols and The Clash?

If buying gifts for others is hard work, once we reach a certain age deciding what we ourselves would like to receive for Christmas is a nightmare. What we really want is something like a shiny new 998cc Honda Fireblade to ease our mid-life crisis, but what we invariably end up with is a gift voucher or bright yellow socks. And we have to appear grateful. 'Oh, thank you so much, I haven't got socks in that shade.'

Socks and vouchers may be boring, but at least they are safe. It's when people with the best of intentions go out on a limb and try to surprise us that we need to be worried. When we tell the donor of some hideous ornament that was purchased because it matches our star sign, 'Oh, you shouldn't have,' we're not just being polite. We really mean it; you should NOT have. Already our mind is fast-forwarding to how we can palm it off on to someone else next year. Go into any major store in the days after Christmas and the longest queue is always at the returns desk. Doesn't that tell us something?

If further proof were needed that Scrooge had

the right idea about Christmas, why is it that as soon as we make an attempt to get into the Christmas spirit by over-indulging in mince pies and sparkling wine – so all we want to do is nod off til 6pm in front of the umpteenth repeat of *Mary Poppins* – someone suggests going for a bracing walk or even a game of charades? What kind of masochists do we share our DNA with?

And if children are present and we are finally enticed out of our comfy chair, we can be sure there will be a stray Lego brick waiting to inflict pain on an unsuspecting, shoeless foot. If only we owned a nice thick pair of socks.

Ultimately, all most of us can do with Christmas is grin and bear it, rather like a trip to the dentist, consoling ourselves with the fact that it will soon be over and the pain will be gone.

This collection of festive jokes is presented in the hope that it might just bring a fleeting moment of light relief from the annual ordeal that is Christmas, and allow the merest hint of a smile to cross even the stoniest face. But we realize that is a lot to ask.

Bah humbug!

THE TRUE
MEANING OF
CHRISTMAS

One Christmas Eve, as the tree lights in the lounge shone brightly while snow fell outside, the youngest boy in the family was overcome by the magic of the moment. Gazing up in awe at the twinkling decorations, he asked his father: 'Dad, how did the fairy get on top of the Christmas tree?'

The father replied: 'You want to know how the fairy got on top of the Christmas tree, son? Well, I'll tell you the story of how that happened. Once upon a time, there was a fairy who was helping Santa Claus by decorating his grotto in time for Christmas. But Santa was in a bad mood. He had been let down by two of the reindeer, Mrs Claus was giving him a hard time and he had been drinking heavily. So the last thing he was interested in was decorating his grotto. He just couldn't be bothered. But the fairy was really enthusiastic and wanted everything to look as pretty as possible for the children.

"Santa, what shall I do with this gold tinsel?" asked the fairy politely.

"I don't know," growled Santa. "And I don't care either."

A few minutes later, the fairy appeared with a box of lovely silver balls.

"Santa, what shall I do with these beautiful silver balls?" asked the fairy.

"Oh, do what you like with them!" hissed Santa dismissively.

A few minutes later, the fairy appeared with a Christmas tree.

"Santa, what shall I do with this splendid Christmas tree?" asked the fairy.

That was the last straw for Santa. He turned to the fairy and yelled: "As far as I'm concerned, you can stick it up your ..."

And that, son, is how the fairy got on top of the Christmas tree.'

On Christmas morning, a father asked his four-year-old son: 'Did you see Father Christmas this year?'

'No,' replied the boy, 'it was too dark to see him. But I heard what he said when he stubbed his toe on the edge of my bed.'

A Mafia godfather's grandson was writing his Christmas list to Jesus. He started: 'Dear baby Jesus, I have been a good boy all year, so I want a ...'

Then he looked at it, had second thoughts, scrunched the letter into a ball and threw it in the bin.

Taking a new piece of paper, he started again: 'Dear baby Jesus, I have been a good boy for most of the year, so I want a ...'

Again, he decided it didn't sound right, so he crumpled the paper into a ball and threw it in the bin.

Then he had an idea. He went into his mother's room, grabbed a statue of the Virgin Mary, put it in a solid wooden desk and locked the drawer.

Taking another piece of paper, he wrote: 'Dear baby Jesus, if you ever want to see your mother again ...'

What is different about the
Italian-American
version of Christmas?

~

One Mary, one Jesus and
thirty-three wise guys.

A young couple were touring the Holy Land over the festive period and thought that it would be wonderful if they could spend Christmas Eve in Bethlehem, the birthplace of Jesus. Despite not booking in advance, they were sure they would be able to find somewhere to stay – no matter how basic the accommodation.

Arriving in the town late in the afternoon, they spent hours searching for a suitable hotel or guest house, but to no avail. Finally, they showed up at the White Horse, Bethlehem, a large and expensive coaching inn. It was pretty much their last hope.

Leaving his wife outside, the man went up to reception, but the woman behind the desk informed him that all their rooms were taken and that they would probably not be able to find anywhere in the whole of Bethlehem that night. 'It's Christmas Eve,' she explained. 'It's our busiest time of the year.'

No matter how much the couple offered to pay for a room, the receptionist still maintained that she had none available.

In a last act of desperation, the man said: 'I bet if I told you my name was Joseph, that the woman waiting in the car was called Mary, and that she had a newborn infant, you would find us a room for the night?'

'Er... well,' stammered the receptionist. 'I suppose if that were the case I might...'

'Well,' he said, 'I guarantee you they're not coming tonight, so we'll take their room!'

A millionaire was driving along in his stretch limo when he saw a humble man eating grass by the roadside. Ordering his driver to stop, he wound down the window and called to the man: 'Why are you eating grass?'

'Because, sir, we don't have enough money to buy real food.'

'Come with me then,' said the millionaire.

'But, sir, I have a wife, four sisters and seven children.'

'That's OK – bring them all along.'

The man and his large family climbed into the limo. 'Sir, you are too kind, taking pity on us at Christmas. You truly embody the spirit of the season. How can I ever thank you for taking all of us with you, for offering us a new home?'

'No, you don't understand,' said the millionaire. 'The grass at my home is three feet high. No lawnmower will cut it.'

Why is Mrs Claus always checking Santa's phone?

~

Because he seems to know where all the naughty girls live.

Three men drank so much on Christmas Eve that they died and found themselves at the pearly gates, waiting to enter heaven, where St Peter told them they had to present something associated with Christmas.

The first man searched through his pockets and found some mistletoe, so he was admitted to heaven. The second man presented a cracker, so he too was allowed in. The third man produced a pair of ladies' pants.

Confused by this last gesture, St Peter asked: 'How do these represent Christmas?'

The man replied: 'They're Carol's.'

The three wise men arrived in Bethlehem to visit the child lying in the manger. One of the wise men was exceptionally tall and, as he entered the stable, he bumped his head on the low doorway. 'Jesus Christ!' he exclaimed.

'Quick, Mary, write that down,' said Joseph. 'It's better than Wayne.'

While playing Joseph in the school nativity play, a young boy forgot his lines. He was quickly prompted from the side by a teacher who whispered: 'You have travelled a very long way, Joseph. You are hot and tired. What do you think you would say to the innkeeper?'

Joseph brightened up, wiped his brow and said loudly: 'Boy, do I need a drink!'

'In the school nativity play, I was always picked to play Bethlehem.'
JO BRAND

Why is Christmas just like a day at the office?

~

Because you do all the work and the fat guy in the suit gets all the credit.

A museum in a small Texas town displayed a nativity scene that had obviously been created with a great amount of skill, craftsmanship and patience. However, one small feature bothered a man visiting from New York: the three wise men were all wearing firemen's helmets. Unable to think of any explanation for it, the visitor decided to ask the woman behind the counter at the museum gift shop.

She immediately exploded into a rage: 'You Yankees never do read the Bible!'

The visitor assured her that he did, but said that he simply couldn't remember any reference to firemen in the Good Book.

Pulling her copy of the Bible from behind the counter, she flicked impatiently through some pages before jabbing her finger at a passage. Sticking it in his face, she said: 'See, it says right here, "The three wise men came from afar."'

A little boy went to Santa's grotto. Santa said:
'And what would you like for Christmas?'
The little boy said: 'I want to be a grown-up.'
'OK,' said Santa. 'That's not a problem. In fact,
shall we start now? **I'M NOT REAL!!'**

Instead of a traditional nativity play at Christmas, a school decided to stage a modern interpretation with a cast of five-year-olds. The female teacher who was doing the casting was a keen student of drama and method acting. When auditioning young Timmy for a part, she said: 'Now, Timmy, I want you to communicate your thoughts.'

Timmy looked at her blankly. 'Communicate my thoughts? I have no idea what that means.'

'Perfect,' said the teacher. 'You can play the husband.'

It was just before Christmas and two hobos were sitting on a park bench in Dublin. One was holding a cross and the other a Star of David. Both had hats positioned in front of them to accept money from the numerous shoppers who were passing by.

A local priest, Father O'Flynn, watched as the shoppers totally ignored the man with the Star of David, but gave generously to the man holding the cross. Before long, the hat in front of the man with the cross was full of coins, but the hat in front of the man with the Star of David was empty.

Eventually, Father O'Flynn went over to the men and said to the one with the Star of David: 'Don't you realize this is a Catholic country? You'll never get any contributions holding a Star of David.'

The man with the Star of David turned to the one holding the cross and said: 'Hymie, can you believe this guy is trying to tell us how to run our business?!'

In the worst winter in decades, thousands of homes were cut off by deep snowdrifts over Christmas, including a family living in a remote mountain cabin in Canada. After three months of no contact with the outside world, the family became the subject of a Red Cross rescue mission.

For weeks even the Red Cross team were unable to force their way through to the cabin, which by now was almost completely buried in snow. Finally, in an act of selfless determination, the brave rescuers succeeded in hacking out a path to the cabin. Not knowing what they would find, they knocked on the front door. After a minute or so, the father of the family answered the door.

'Red Cross,' announced the leader of the team.

'Sorry,' said the father. 'It's been such a tough winter that I don't think we can give anything this year.'

Appearing on a TV game show, a contestant only needed to answer one more question to win $500,000. 'To be today's champion and win the prize of a lifetime,' the host smiled, ramping up the tension, 'name two of Santa's reindeer.'

The contestant looked relieved. 'I know this,' she said. 'Rudolph and ... Olive.'

The studio audience began to murmur ominously. The host put a consoling arm around the contestant's shoulder and said: 'We can accept Rudolph, but I'm afraid Olive is incorrect.'

'It can't be,' said the contestant. 'It's in the song.'

'What song?'

'You know,' she said, and began to sing: 'Rudolph the red-nosed reindeer had a very shiny nose. And if you ever saw it, you would even say it glows. Olive the other reindeer ...'

What did Santa call his reindeer
that couldn't fly?

~

Dinner.

A newspaper editor was furious. 'Who checked for typos in the online story promoting the Christmas grotto at the department store?' he yelled.

'I did,' said a junior reporter meekly. 'Why? Is there a problem?'

'I'll say there is,' said the editor. 'I've just had the store on the phone. Our story tells parents that they should bring their children along to the grotto to have their photo taken with Satan!'

Three-year-old Ruth had been fighting a lot with her older sister all year. Her parents tried to put a stop to the bickering by telling Ruth that Santa Claus was watching.

'He doesn't like children fighting, especially with their sisters,' they warned, 'so if your behaviour doesn't improve he might not be bringing any toys to this house at Christmas.' However, their words had little effect and the fighting continued.

Eventually, Ruth became so disruptive that her mother made the ultimate threat: 'I'm calling Santa to tell him what a naughty girl you've been.'

Ruth's eyes grew big as her mother phoned Santa (in reality Ruth's Uncle Peter) and told him how Ruth had been misbehaving. After a minute or so, she handed the phone to Ruth, saying: 'Santa wants to talk to you.'

Santa explained to her how children who fought with their sisters would not be receiving any presents this year. He would be watching, he said, and he expected things to be better from now on.

Ruth nodded at each of Santa's remarks before silently putting the phone down. Certain that her ruse had worked, the mother asked her: 'What did Santa say to you?'

In a hushed voice, Ruth said gloomily: 'Santa said he won't be bringing any toys to my sister this year.'

Just before Christmas, Santa Claus, an honest politician and a compassionate lawyer were taking the lift of a five-star hotel. Just before the doors opened, all three spotted a £20 note lying on the floor. Which one picked it up?

Santa, of course, because the other two don't exist.

Two blondes drove all the way to a Norwegian forest in search of a Christmas tree. They had prepared for the trip right down to the last detail, wearing sensible, warm winter clothing, including fur hats and thick snow boots. They also made sure to take the necessary equipment and carried a saw, a hatchet and rope so that they could drag the Christmas tree of their choice back to their car. Nothing had been left to chance.

They were so determined to find the perfect Christmas tree that their search went on for hours, even in the face of a driving blizzard. Finally, as fatigue and darkness began to set in, one blonde turned to the other and said: 'I give up! I've had enough of this! There are hundreds of beautiful Christmas trees all around us. Let's just cut one down whether it's decorated or not.'

'I never believed in Santa Claus because I knew no white dude would come into my neighbourhood after dark.'
DICK GREGORY

A little boy went into Santa's grotto at the city centre store.

'And what would you like for Christmas, young man?' asked the jolly Santa.

'Could you please send me a baby sister?' said the little boy sweetly.

'I'll do my best,' said Santa, 'if you send me your mother.'

To build a manger for his son's nativity scene, a man went to a hardware store and asked for some nails.
'How long do you want them?' asked the sales assistant.
'Oh,' said the customer. 'I was rather hoping to keep them.'

It was Christmas Eve, and a little old lady was sitting all alone, except for her cat, in a tiny house, huddled up for warmth in front of the fire. Then suddenly there was a flash of light and a fairy appeared in the room.

'I am your good fairy,' she announced. 'I can see that you are poor and alone at Christmas, so I have the power to grant you three wishes.'

Before the old woman had a chance to speak, the fairy added: 'Don't be too hasty with your wishes. Give them careful thought because you will get exactly what you wish for, and no wish can be amended afterwards.'

The old woman looked at her threadbare clothing and grim surroundings and said: 'My first wish is to be extremely wealthy.'

Poof! The small house was instantly transformed into a golden palace, and her clothes were the finest designer labels.

'Now what is your second wish?' asked the fairy.

'I wish I was twenty-one and beautiful again,' said the old woman.

Poof! The old woman's wrinkled skin became smooth and soft, and her grey hair became long and blonde. She looked sixty years younger.

'And what is your third, final wish?' asked the fairy.

The old woman said: 'I would like you to change my cat into a handsome prince who will love me and take care of me for the rest of my life.'

Poof! And the cat was replaced by a handsome, young prince. He reached out to the woman, pulled her to her feet and kissed her passionately. Then he gazed longingly into her eyes and said: 'I bet you're sorry you had me neutered now!'

A man who hated Christmas with a vengeance was always particularly irritated by the groups of carol singers who would appear uninvited on his doorstep, sing a few tuneless bars of 'Silent Night' and then demand money. So when his doorbell rang for the umpteenth time that December, he instead sent his son to the answer the door.

The boy came back and said: 'Dad, there's someone at the door collecting donations for a local swimming pool.'

'OK,' said the father, full of seasonal meanness. 'Give him a glass of water!'

How did the miser celebrate Christmas
at his house?

~

He installed a parking meter
on the roof.

One November, a Native American tribe asked their chief whether the impending Christmas period was going to be cold. He did not really know the answer but said that, in all probability, it would be cold, and he advised the members of the village to stock up on supplies of firewood. Not wishing to leave anything to chance and being ever considerate of the welfare of his people, the chief then phoned the National Weather Service and asked: 'Is this Christmas going to be cold?'

'Yes, quite cold,' answered the meteorologist.

Hearing this, the chief urged his people to intensify the collection of firewood.

A week later, he called the National Weather Service again. 'Is it going to be a *very* cold Christmas?' he asked.

'Yes,' replied the meteorologist. 'It looks like it's going to be a very cold Christmas indeed.'

Armed with this information, the chief now told his villagers to find every last scrap of firewood available.

Two weeks later, he phoned the National Weather Service once more and asked: 'Are you *absolutely* certain this Christmas is going to be very cold?'

'Absolutely sure,' replied the meteorologist. 'The Indians are collecting firewood like crazy!'

A school principal paid a farmer one hundred dollars for a donkey to use in that year's nativity play. The farmer agreed to deliver the donkey the next day but, when he drove up in his truck, he had some bad news.

'Sorry,' he said. 'The donkey died.'

'Oh. Well, can I have my money back?' asked the principal.

'Can't do that,' said the farmer. 'I've already spent it.'

'OK then, just unload the donkey.'

'What are you going to do with him?'

'I'm going to raffle him off,' said the principal.

'You can't raffle off a dead donkey!' the farmer protested.

'Sure I can. I just won't tell anyone he's dead.'

A month later, the principal bumped into the farmer again. The farmer asked: 'What happened with the dead donkey?'

'I raffled him off among the schoolchildren's parents, just like I said I would. I sold 500 tickets at two dollars apiece and made a profit for the school of $998 dollars.'

'Didn't anyone complain?'

'Only the guy who won,' said the principal. 'So I gave him back his two dollars.'

A little boy climbed onto Santa's lap in the Christmas grotto.

'And what would you like for Christmas?' asked Santa.

The boy stared at him in disbelief and said: 'Didn't you get my email?'

*What is the surest proof that Microsoft
has a monopoly?*

~

**Santa Claus has had to switch from
Chimneys to Windows.**

Sitting alone on a park bench in the depths of December, a man was contemplating his woes when Father Christmas suddenly appeared at his side. 'Don't look so troubled,' said Father Christmas. 'This is meant to be a joyous time of the year when everyone is jolly like me.'

'But I've had a lousy couple of months,' explained the man. 'I might lose my house, my job, everything.'

'Fret no more,' said Father Christmas. 'Since

this is the festive season I am allowed to grant three wishes. So I propose granting you two wishes and, if you don't mind, I'll keep the last wish for myself.'

'That sounds more than fair,' said the man.

'Now what is your first wish?' asked Father Christmas.

The man thought for a moment before saying: 'My first wish would be to have three million pounds a year for the rest of my life.'

'No problem,' said Father Christmas. 'Your wish will be granted. And what is your second wish?'

'I would like to live to over a hundred,' said the man.

'Consider it done,' said Father Christmas. 'And now for my wish. It's not easy attracting women in this red suit and with the constant stench of reindeer poo in the air. What with the unsociable hours I work, it's extraordinarily difficult to maintain a relationship. As a result I haven't had sex for ages. So if you're OK with it, I'd like to sleep with your wife.'

The man gave the suggestion quick consideration and replied: 'Why not? It seems only right. After all, I'm going to be getting all that money and a long life. I guess it's the least I can do in return. I'll drive you to my home now.'

When they arrived at his house, the man explained the deal to his wife. Father Christmas then took her upstairs and ravished her for two hours, it was the best sex she'd ever had. Eventually, in a state of total exhaustion, he turned to her and asked: 'How old is your husband?'

'Forty-two,' she replied breathlessly.

'And he still believes in Father Christmas?'

What would have happened if it had been three wise women instead of wise men? They would have asked for directions, arrived on time, helped deliver the baby, cleaned the stable, made a casserole, and brought practical gifts. But what would they have said as they left?

'That baby doesn't look anything like Joseph!'

'Virgin, my arse! I knew her in school!'

'Can you believe they let all those disgusting animals in there?'

'I heard that Joseph isn't even working right now.'

'I bet you'll have a long wait before you get your casserole dish back.'

FIVE REASONS WHY SANTA CLAUS MUST BE A MAN

1. He turns up late.
2. He drinks your booze and eats your food.
3. He only comes once.
4. He clears off before you wake up.
5. He wears the same outfit year after year – something no woman would ever do.

AND FIVE REASONS WHY SANTA CLAUS COULD BE A WOMAN

1. Most men don't even think about selecting gifts until Christmas Eve.
2. Men can't pack a bag.
3. Men would inevitably get lost in the snow and clouds, and then refuse to stop and ask for directions.
4. Men are only interested in stockings when someone is wearing them.
5. No man would be seen dead in a red velvet suit.

A simple country guy wanted to join an amateur baseball team. The coach looked him over and decided to give him a chance but said that first he had to pass an intelligence test.

'I'll give you three questions,' said the coach. 'If you come back in a week and answer all three correctly, you're on the team. The first question is, how many days of the week start with the letter T? Second, how many seconds are there in a year? And third, how many D's are there in "Rudolph the Red-Nosed Reindeer"?'

A week later, the country guy returned, confident that he had the correct answers. 'OK,' said the coach, 'question one: how many days of the week start with T?'

'Two,' replied the guy.

'Very good,' said the coach. 'What are they?'

'Today and tomorrow.'

'Hmmm . . . OK, I'll let you have that. So question two: how many seconds are there in a year?'

'Twelve.'

'Twelve? How did you come up with *twelve*?'

'Well,' explained the guy, 'there's the second of January, the second of February, the second of . . .'

'OK, OK. Third question: how many D's in

"Rudolph the Red-Nosed Reindeer"?'

'Oh, that's easy,' laughed the guy. 'Two hundred and twenty.'

'What!' exclaimed the coach. 'How did you get that figure?'

To which the country guy started singing: 'Dee-dee dee-dee-dee dee-dee . . .'

A doctor was examining his last patient on Christmas Eve. It was a mother and her nineteen-year-old daughter who had apparently been displaying unusual symptoms. These included a significant increase in weight, sickness most mornings and strange food cravings.

The doctor checked the daughter over and announced that, without a shadow of doubt, she was pregnant.

'Don't be so ridiculous,' protested the mother. 'She can't be. She has never been with a man.'

The girl confirmed that what her mother said was true, and claimed that she had never even so much as kissed a man.

The doctor gave the girl a quizzical look and

then quietly walked over to the window and began staring out of it.

'Is something wrong?' asked the mother.

'No, not really,' replied the doctor. 'It's just that the last time something like this happened a bright star appeared in the east and three wise men came over the hill. I'll be damned if I'm going to miss it this time!'

PARTY POOPERS

At the end of the office Christmas party, a middle manager had drunk far more than was good for him. He staggered out of the bar, swaying and stumbling, barely able to put one foot in front of the other. He eventually managed to reach his car but, just as he was about to try and unlock the door, a police officer tapped him on the shoulder and said: 'I hope you're not thinking of driving tonight, sir?'

'Of course I am,' he answered. 'I'm in no fit state to walk!'

On their way home from a pre-Christmas party at a friend's house, a wife turned to her husband and said: 'Have I ever told you how sexy and irresistible to women you are?'

'I don't believe you have,' he replied, flattered.

'Then what in hell's name gave you that idea at the party?'

'Christmas begins about 1 December with an office party and ends when you finally realize what you spent, around 15 April the next year.'
P.J. O'ROURKE

An old man called the police to complain about the Christmas party that was taking place at a neighbour's house. 'The behaviour at number twenty-seven has been absolutely disgraceful,' he moaned to the officer. 'There have been naked young women wandering around in there with the curtains wide open.'

The officer looked through the window. 'But I can't even see number twenty-seven from here,' he said.

'No,' said the old man. 'You have to climb on the dresser in the bedroom, stand on tiptoe and look through the skylight.'

A man tried to get into a works Christmas party at a city bar. It was a fancy dress event and he was dressed as a pair of jump leads. After a bit of an argument, the doorman said: 'OK, you can go in, but don't start anything.'

Despite the fact that it was the day of the office Christmas party, the boss decided that one of his young employees had been taking too many liberties of late. It was time to lay down the law to him.

The boss called him into his office and said firmly: 'Your appalling timekeeping is getting worse by the day, and it hasn't gone unnoticed by your co-workers. I've heard them muttering among themselves about how you roll in through the door at least fifteen minutes late every morning. It has to stop. Have you any suggestions?'

'Yes,' said the young man. 'Is there another door I could use?'

Norman from Accounts was definitely not a party person, and almost had to be dragged along to the company's annual Christmas bash.

'Why don't you like parties?' asked Emma, his colleague. 'I thought everyone loved a good party.'

'I think it dates back to a couple of family weddings I attended in my twenties,' he explained. 'All of my aunts and grandmothers would come up to me, poke me in the ribs and squawk gleefully: "You're next! You're next!"'

'I can understand why you might find that irritating,' agreed Emma.

'It was,' continued Norman. 'Mind you, they stopped after I started doing the same thing to them at family funerals.'

After drinking one sherry too many at their office Christmas party, Jean, a middle-aged spinster, leaned over to Colin, one of the senior partners, and whispered: 'What would it take for you to kiss me under the mistletoe?'

He shot back: 'Anaesthetic.'

Sam and Will, two workers in the City of London, staggered out of their company's Christmas party. Sam crossed the street while Will stumbled down the steps of a London Underground station. When Sam reached the other side of the street, he saw Will emerging from the station stairs.

'Where have you been?' asked Sam.

'I don't know,' said Will, 'but you should see the train set that guy has in his basement!'

'You moon the wrong person at an office party, and suddenly you're not "professional" anymore.'
JEFF FOXWORTHY

A man was sitting in a bar when he noticed a group of people wearing Christmas party hats and using sign language. He also saw that the bartender was using sign language to speak to them. 'They're regular customers,' explained the bartender, 'and they taught me how to sign.'

'That's fantastic,' said the man. 'Most people wouldn't have made the effort.'

A few minutes later, the group began waving their arms around while signing wildly. The bartender looked over and signed: 'Now cut that out! I warned you!' And he threw them out of the bar.

'What was all that about?' asked the man.

The bartender replied: 'If I told them once, I told them a thousand times – no singing in the bar!'

What do actuaries do to liven up their
office Christmas party?

~

They invite an accountant.

Two office workers wanted to get off early on Christmas Eve so that they could get to the pub. The woman said: 'I can make the boss give me the rest of the day off.'

'How can you do that?' asked her male colleague.

The woman said: 'Just wait and see.'

She then hung herself upside down from the ceiling. When the boss walked in, he said: 'What the hell are you doing?'

'I'm a light bulb,' said the woman.

The boss said: 'You've been working too hard. You've gone crazy. Take the rest of the day off, and Happy Christmas.'

The man started to follow her. 'Where do you think you're going?' demanded the boss.

The man said: 'I'm going home, too. I can't work in the dark.'

A couple visited a neighbour's house for a Christmas party. The following morning the wife was in a foul mood. She told her husband firmly: 'You certainly made a fool of yourself last night. I just hope nobody realized you were sober.'

A man woke up with a terrible hangover on the morning after his office Christmas party. Eventually forcing his eyes open, he noticed two aspirins, a glass of water and a single red rose on his bedside table. Sitting up with a struggle, he then realized that all his clothes had been ironed and laid out immaculately, ready for him to wear.

Puzzled by what was going on, he staggered into the bathroom where a glance in the mirror revealed that he had a black eye. Stuck to the mirror was a note from his wife, which read: 'Breakfast is on the stove. I've gone to the shop to buy groceries for your favourite dinner tonight. All my love, Gemma xxx.'

So he stumbled downstairs to the kitchen where, as promised, there was a hot breakfast, freshly made coffee and his morning newspaper all waiting for him. His son was already at the table.

'Son,' he asked, 'my mind's a bit hazy this morning. Do you know what happened when I came home last night?'

'Well,' said the son, 'you got home at about one in the morning, so drunk you could barely stand. You fell over the coffee table and broke it and then walked straight into the door. That's how you've ended up with a black eye.'

Still confused, the man said: 'So why is your mother making such a fuss of me, being so kind and considerate, tending to my headache, cooking my breakfast, ironing my clothes and even putting a rose at the side of my bed?'

'I have no idea,' replied the son. 'The only other thing I remember is Mum dragging you to the bedroom, and when she tried to take your pants off, you screamed: "Get off me, I'm married!"'

The boss called a team meeting on Christmas Eve and, in keeping with the time of year, he told a joke. Everyone on the team roared with laughter except for one guy who sat there in stony silence.

The boss glared at him and said: 'Didn't you understand my joke?'

'Yes, I understood it,' he replied, 'but I handed in my notice two hours ago.'

At a marketing company's Christmas party, an overweight middle manager went up to an attractive young woman and surprised her by kissing her under the mistletoe.

'What was that?' she asked, horrified.

'Direct marketing!' he beamed.

Then she slapped him hard around the face.

'What was that?' he whined.

'Customer feedback!'

A doctor and a lawyer were chatting at a big civic Christmas party, but their conversation was repeatedly interrupted by people coming up to the doctor and asking him for free medical advice. After putting up with it for the best part of an hour, the exasperated doctor said to the lawyer: 'What do you do to stop people asking you for legal advice when you're out of the office?'

'I give it to them,' replied the lawyer, 'and then I send them a bill.'

'OK,' said the doctor hesitantly. 'It sounds extreme, but I think I might have to give it a try.'

'You should,' said the lawyer, 'and there's no need to feel guilty about it.'

'You're absolutely right,' agreed the doctor, warming to the idea. 'I shouldn't feel guilty. Thank you.'

When the doctor saw his post the next morning, he found a bill from the lawyer.

A guy was really getting into the Christmas spirit at the office party, but he had drunk so much sparkling wine that he began to feel the need to fart. Since the music was loud, he decided to time his farts to the beat of the songs, certain that nobody in the room would notice. So he let a few rip, but then became aware that the whole office was staring at him. That was when he realized he was listening to his iPod.

After drinking steadily for hours, a man staggered out of his company Christmas party and boarded a bus for the journey home. Lurching along the centre gangway, he suddenly stopped and shouted that everyone sitting in the seats to his right was an idiot and that everyone in the seats to his left was an asshole.

Hearing this, a passenger stood up angrily and said: 'How dare you! I'm not an idiot!'

The drunk yelled back: 'So move to the other side then.'

A married man made a move on his new personal assistant at the office Christmas party, and the pair ended up in bed together back at her apartment. Exhausted, they eventually fell asleep and did not wake up until seven o'clock in the evening. When he looked at his phone he saw fifteen missed calls from his wife. Thinking quickly, he threw on his clothes and asked his assistant to take his shoes outside and rub them through the grass and dirt. Even though she was puzzled by the request, she complied and he slipped them on and drove home.

As soon as he arrived home, his wife demanded to know where he had been.

'Sweetheart,' he replied. 'I can't lie to you. After the office party, I went to bed with Erica, my personal assistant. We had sex all afternoon but then fell asleep and didn't wake until seven o'clock.'

The wife glanced down at his shoes and said: 'You liar! You've been playing golf again!'

'What I hate about office Christmas parties is looking for a job the next day.'
PHYLLIS DILLER

A smartly dressed man entered a trendy bar on Christmas Eve and took a seat. The bartender came over and said: 'What can I get you to drink, sir?'

'Nothing, thank you,' replied the man. 'I tried alcohol once, but I didn't like it and I haven't drunk it since.'

The bartender was puzzled but being a friendly sort of guy he pulled a packet of cigarettes from his pocket and offered one to the man. But the man refused.

'Disgusting habit. I'm surprised you're even allowed to smoke in here. I tried smoking once but I didn't like it and I have never smoked since. As a matter of fact, I wouldn't be in here at all except that I'm waiting for my son.'

To which the bartender replied: 'Your only child, I presume?'

On the morning of the office Christmas party, a worried man decided that he had something he finally needed to get off his chest. So he knocked on the boss's door and entered hesitantly. Once inside, he took a deep breath and said: 'Can we talk? I have a problem.'

'There's no such thing as a problem,' boomed the boss. 'I like to think of every problem as an opportunity.'

'OK,' said the man. 'Then I have a serious drinking opportunity.'

A company boss thought that his secretary had started taking things easy at work. Finally he decided to confront her about it. 'Who said that just because I tried to kiss you at last month's Christmas party, it meant that you could neglect your job?'

The secretary replied: 'My lawyer.'

Scrooge was walking his grandson home from a Christmas party. After a few minutes, the boy complained: 'Gramps, it's still a long way back to our house. I'm getting tired. There's a bus stop across the street. Can't we just take the bus home?'

Scrooge recoiled in horror. 'It would cost £5 for the two of us to get the bus home – even with my senior citizens pass! What a waste of money! We'll continue walking.'

But a minute or so later, Scrooge spotted a taxi and stepped into the street to hail it. 'How much would you charge to take us to Manor Avenue?' he asked the driver.

'£20,' replied the taxi driver.

'That's way too much,' said Scrooge. 'We won't be requiring your services, I'm afraid.'

As the empty taxi drove away, the boy turned to Scrooge and said: 'I can't believe you thought that a taxi ride would be cheaper than the bus, Grandpa!'

'Don't be ridiculous,' said Scrooge. 'Of course I didn't.'

'Then why did you bother flagging down the taxi?'

'Foolish boy!' said Scrooge. 'It's a matter of simple economics. We would have saved £5 by not taking the bus, but now we're saving £20 by not taking a taxi!'

A man appeared in court on a charge of vehicle theft. 'Why did you steal the car?' asked the judge.

'Because I needed to get to work for the Christmas party,' replied the defendant.

'Why didn't you take the bus?'

'I don't have a driver's licence for the bus.'

A boss asked one of his employees to work over Christmas. 'I know how much you've probably been looking forward to having a Christmas break with your family and friends,' he said, 'but I really need you in the office on both Christmas Day and Boxing Day. And I'm afraid I won't be able to offer you any extra money or days off in lieu. Sorry, but that's the way it is. Times are tough. I wouldn't ask if it wasn't absolutely necessary.'

'OK,' said the young employee grudgingly, 'but you know that I rely on public transport to get to work, and there aren't many buses over Christmas. So I'll probably be late.'

'That shouldn't be a problem,' said the boss. 'What time do you expect to get here?'

The young man mused: 'Oh, around about 27 December.'

Richard and Ed were enjoying the company Christmas party in a local bar when a pretty young woman from another department passed them by on the way to the toilet. When she was safely out of earshot, Richard said: 'I think she's really nice.'

'Well, don't be shy,' said Ed. 'Go over and give her the old patter.'

'The patter?' queried Richard, who was not as experienced with women as his friend was.

'Yes, the patter,' repeated Ed.

'But I don't know any patter,' said Richard. 'I've never found it easy to talk to women.'

'Oh, come on!' said Ed despairingly. 'It's easy. All you have to do is say "hello" and she will say "hello". Then you say, "It's a nice place this, isn't it?" Then she will say, "Yes, it is." Then you say, "But not half as nice as you!" Then she will say, "Oh, thank you." And after that the patter will just flow. Look, there she is now, coming back out of the toilet. Go and give it a try.'

Nervously, Richard headed towards the young woman, all the while re-running the patter routine in his head. He walked up to her and said: 'Hello.'

'Hello.'

'It's a nice place this, isn't it?'

'Yes, it is.'

'But not half as nice as you!'

'Oh, thank you.'

There followed a few seconds of uneasy silence, eventually broken by Richard asking in his most nonchalant manner: 'Been for a dump, then?'

The boss showed up for the Christmas party driving a top-of-the range Ferrari.

'Wow!' said one of his junior employees. 'That's an amazing car.'

'Well,' said the boss, 'if you work hard, put all your hours in and strive for excellence I'll be able to afford another one next year.'

Deciding that he wanted to look his best for the office Christmas party, a man called into a barber's shop for a shave and a shoe-shine. While the barber lathered his face and sharpened the straight-edge razor, a beautiful woman knelt down and began to shine the customer's shoes.

After a minute or so, the customer told her: 'You really are gorgeous. I reckon you and I should book a hotel room later.'

'My husband wouldn't like that,' she replied.

'Just tell him you're working overtime,' suggested the customer.

'You tell him,' she said. 'He's the one with the razor.'

In order to let his wife concentrate on the Christmas preparations, a man took his young daughter into the office on Christmas Eve. For part of the time he left her in the care of an employee in an adjoining office so that he could finish off a few things before the festive break. When they arrived back home in the evening, his daughter said to him: 'I saw you in your office with your secretary. Why do you call her a doll?'

Feeling the ferocity of his wife's gaze, he replied carefully: 'My secretary works very hard and is extremely efficient. I'd be lost without her. I guess I call her a doll as a sign of my appreciation.'

'Oh,' said the daughter, 'I thought it was because she closed her eyes when you laid her down on the couch.'

An office manager had too much to drink at the company Christmas party and embarrassed himself in front of his boss. His wife told him the awful truth the following morning.

'Your behaviour was dreadful,' she said. 'At one point you went up to your boss and started jabbing him in the stomach and verbally abusing him. You were swearing like a trooper.'

'Really?' said the husband, shocked.

'Yes,' said the wife. 'You certainly told him what you thought of him. He was furious.'

'Well,' said the husband, in a display of bravado, 'it serves him right. It's about time he heard a few home truths. He's an asshole. Piss on him!'

'You did,' said the wife, 'and he fired you.'

'Well, screw him!'

'I did,' said the wife. 'You're back at work on Monday.'

Even though it was Christmas Eve, the new CEO was determined that nobody in the company was going to slacken off. In fact, he had been appointed chiefly to address the culture of laziness and complacency that had developed within the firm. So when he spotted a young guy leaning against the wall doing nothing, he decided to make an example of him there and then, in front of the whole office.

He walked over to the young man and boomed: 'How much money do you make a week?'

Unfazed, the young man looked at him and replied: 'Um ... £200. Why?'

The CEO then handed him £200 in cash and yelled: 'Right, here's a week's pay. Now get out and don't come back!'

Feeling pretty good about his first firing, the CEO looked around the room and asked: 'Anyone know what that slacker did here?'

'Yes,' one of the workers said: 'Pizza delivery guy.'

SHOP TILL YOU DROP

A New York City mother took her young son to Bloomingdale's department store to meet Santa.

'What would you like for Christmas, young man?' asked the jolly, bearded Santa.

'A PlayStation PS4 console, a bicycle and a new phone,' replied the boy.

'Well, I'll try my best to see that you're lucky,' said Santa.

Later that day, the mother took the boy to

Macy's department store where again they visited Santa's grotto.

'What do you hope to get for Christmas, young man?' asked the Santa.

'A PlayStation PS4 console, a bicycle and a new phone,' replied the boy.

'Are you going to be a good boy and help your mother?' asked Santa.

The boy turned to his mother and said: 'Let's go back to Bloomingdale's. I didn't have to make any promises there.'

While his wife did some last-minute baking, in a moment of weakness a man reluctantly agreed to do the Christmas Eve supermarket shop. He hated every minute but decided that if he added a few treats to the items on the list it might make the exercise almost bearable.

By the time he reached the checkout he was still grumpy but his trolley was overflowing. Behind him in the queue was a little old lady with just a loaf of bread and a packet of butter in her basket.

He turned to her and said: 'Is that all you've got, love?'

Her face brightened. 'Yes, dear,' she said and started to edge forward in hope.

'Well,' he said, 'if I were you, I'd find a seat because I'm going to be ages here.'

On a sunny December day, a father and his young son took a break from Christmas shopping to sit in the park and watch the ducks on the pond. Looking up at the sky and watching the wisps of cloud float gently overhead, the boy turned to his father and said: 'Dad, why are we here?'

'That's a good question, son. I think we're here to enjoy days such as this, to experience nature in all its majesty, the vastness of the sky, the beauty of the trees, the songs of the birds, the rippling flow of the water.

'We're here to help make the world a better place, to pass on our wisdom to future generations who will hopefully profit from our achievements and learn from our mistakes. We're here to savour the small triumphs of life, like passing your school exams, the birth of a new member of the family or a promotion at work.

'And we're here to comfort those dearest to us in times of distress, to provide care and compassion, to offer support and strength, to let them know that no matter how bad a situation may seem they are not alone. Does that answer your question, son?'

'Not really, Dad.'

'No?'

'No, what I meant was, why are we here when Mum said to pick her up outside the supermarket forty-five minutes ago?'

> *'Why is it that when snooty department stores put their Christmas decorations out just after the fourth of July it's "elegant foresight", but when I leave my Christmas lights up until April, my neighbours think I'm just tacky?'*
> ALISA MEADOWS

A man was complaining to his friend that his wife kept asking him for more money to spend on Christmas preparations. 'A month ago she asked me for £100, two weeks ago she said she wanted £200 and yesterday it was £400.'

'What does she do with it all?' asked the friend.

'I don't know. I never give her any.'

John only went to the supermarket once a year – and that was on 24 December for the big Christmas shop. As he toured the aisles, he noticed a pretty blonde woman waving to him and mouthing 'hello'. To his consternation, he couldn't place her. So when he caught up with her, he asked her tentatively: 'Do you know me?'

'I think you're the father of one of my kids,' she replied.

He began to panic. His mind raced back to the only time he had ever been unfaithful to his wife and he blurted out: 'My God, are you the stripper from the 2011 J. Brown & Co. Christmas party who got me so worked up we had to sneak into a back room and have wild sex on the pool table while my colleagues sprayed whipped cream on us?'

'No,' she replied calmly. 'I'm your son's science teacher.'

A man was admiring the model train sets at a major toyshop on Christmas Eve. Eventually, he said to the sales assistant: 'That's amazing. I'll buy it.'

The assistant agreed: 'Yes, it is impressive. I'm sure your son will love it.'

'You're probably right,' said the man. 'In that case I'll take two.'

An elderly gentleman walked into an upmarket jewellery shop with the intention of buying a diamond bracelet for his wife for Christmas. As he bent over to study it more closely in the cabinet, he inadvertently broke wind. Hugely embarrassed, he prayed that nobody would realize what he had done and that no sales assistant would suddenly approach him. But as he turned around, he saw a smartly dressed member of staff standing right behind him.

'How may I help you today, sir?' asked the sales assistant, exuding professionalism.

Still desperately hoping that his little accident had gone undetected, the old man asked nervously: 'How much is the diamond bracelet?'

The assistant replied: 'Sir, if you farted just looking at it, you're going to crap yourself when I tell you the price!'

A small boy got lost in a mall while Christmas shopping with his mother. Remembering what she had always told him, he went up to a police officer and said: 'Officer, did you happen to see a lady without a boy like me?'

An elderly man got in his car and drove to the mall to do some Christmas shopping. Usually he took the back route but being in a hurry he chose a motorway with which he was not familiar. His wife stayed at home watching daytime TV. Suddenly there was a newsflash and the announcer said: 'Take care on the motorway this afternoon because there is a motorist driving the wrong way!'

Knowing that was the route her husband was taking, she called him on his cell phone to warn him that someone was driving the wrong way on the motorway. 'Tell me about it!' he replied. 'And it's not just one car. There's hundreds of them!'

Two friends were talking about what they were getting their partners for Christmas. 'We're not spending much on each other this year,' said one. 'Finances are a bit tight, so I just bought her a small bottle of perfume.'

'Oh, I bought a barge pole,' said the other. 'Thought I'd push the boat out.'

'From a commercial point of view, if Christmas did not exist it would be necessary to invent it.'
Katharine Whitehorn

With a reduced bus service operating over the Christmas period, two elderly ladies were left waiting a long time at the bus stop. One said: 'I hate it when I have to wait ages for a bus. I've been sitting here so long that my butt has fallen asleep.'

'I know,' said the other. 'I heard it snoring.'

A young woman went shopping for a dress to wear at a New Year's party. She asked the shop assistant: 'Can I try on that dress in the window?'

'Certainly not,' said the assistant. 'You'll have to use the fitting room like everyone else.'

An attractive young woman was shopping for fabric in the week before Christmas. Having made her choice, she asked the young man behind the counter: 'How much is this material per metre?'

Pointing to the mistletoe hanging above the counter, he smiled and said: 'You're in luck. We have a special offer this week: one kiss per metre.'

'OK,' she said, 'I'll take thirteen metres.'

With anticipation etched all over his face, he quickly measured out the fabric, wrapped it and handed it to the pretty, young woman. As he edged forward ready for the kisses, she called to an old lady who was browsing at the adjoining counter and said: 'My grandma will pay the bill.'

With shoppers eager to snap up a bargain, a long queue had formed at eight o'clock in the morning for a store's big Boxing Day sale. As opening time approached, a small man pushed his way to the front of the line but was quickly jostled to the back again by angry shoppers who told him: 'No queue jumping, pal! Wait your turn like everybody else!'

Moments later he tried once more, forcing his way to the front, only to be thrown to the back of the queue again by shoppers telling him: 'Are you deaf, pal? Try that again and you'll be needing an ambulance!'

Straightening his tie and recovering his composure, he told the person at the back of the line: 'That does it! If they do that again, I refuse to open the store!'

A man went to a store to buy a Christmas tree.
The sales assistant said: 'Are you going to put it
up yourself?'
'No,' said the man. 'I was thinking
the living room.'

While out Christmas shopping on a windy December day, an old man spotted an elderly lady standing on a street corner, holding on to her hat for dear life while her coat and dress billowed all around her.

Going over to her, he said: 'Lady, you should be ashamed of yourself, standing here in the street in public, allowing the wind to blow your coat and dress almost over your head so that everyone can see your bits, and all the while you're holding that damn hat with both hands! It's not ladylike!'

'Listen, Mr Busybody,' she snapped. 'Everything down there is eighty-three years old, but this hat is brand new!'

Two weeks before Christmas, an employee went to see his boss.

'Boss,' he said, 'my wife wants me to go Christmas shopping with her next week. Is there any chance I could have a day off?'

'I'm sorry,' said the boss, 'but we're short-handed at the moment. There's no way I can give you a day off next week. I'm afraid your wife will have to do the Christmas shopping by herself.'

The man breathed a sigh of relief. 'Thanks, boss, I knew I could rely on you!'

After stocking up on Christmas groceries, a little old lady was stopped by security as she left the store. The next day she found herself in court charged with shoplifting. Her husband watched from the public gallery.

The judge asked her what she had stolen.

'A can of peaches, Your Honour,' she replied.

'And how many peaches were in the can?' asked the judge.

'Six, Your Honour.'

'Very well,' said the judge. 'Although this is not your first offence, I am feeling lenient at this time of year, so I sentence you to spend one day in jail for each peach that you stole – that's a total of six days in jail.'

The judge then asked if anyone present had anything they wished to say, at which point her husband called out: 'She stole a can of peas, too!'

While doing the big Christmas shop at his local supermarket, a man noticed an old lady following him around the aisles. Whenever he stopped, she stopped, too. Furthermore, she kept staring at him. She finally overtook him just before the checkout where she turned to him and said: 'I hope I haven't made you feel uncomfortable, but you look so much like my late son.'

'That's OK,' he said.

'I know it's silly,' she continued, 'but if you could possibly bring yourself to call out "Goodbye, Mother" as I leave, it would mean so much to me.'

The old lady duly passed through the cash desk and, as she left the supermarket, the man called out, 'Goodbye, Mother' as requested. The old lady waved back and smiled warmly.

Pleased that he had managed to add a little sunshine to someone's day, the man went to pay for his groceries.

'That comes to £98.'

'What?' he squawked. 'I haven't bought that much!'

'I can see that, but your mother said you'd pay for her.'

A man went into a toyshop to buy a Christmas present for his five-year-old daughter. 'What dolls do you have?' he asked the assistant.

She said: 'We have Barbie, Sindy, Tressy – her hair really grows – teen doll, schoolgirl doll and neurotic doll.'

'Neurotic doll? What's that?' he asked.

The assistant explained: 'It's wound up already.'

A woman was picking through the frozen turkeys at the supermarket, but couldn't find one big enough to cater for her entire family at Christmas. So she asked a passing member of staff: 'Do these turkeys get any bigger?'

'No, madam,' he replied. 'They're dead.'

A man decided to treat himself to a new pair of shoes for Christmas. So he went into the local shoe shop and asked for a pair, size eight.

Glancing at the customer's large feet, the sales assistant said: 'Are you sure, sir? You look like a size eleven to me.'

'Just bring me a size eight,' he insisted.

So, despite his misgivings, the assistant fetched a pair of size eights and the customer squeezed both feet into them, wincing with pain at the effort. He then stood up, although his acute discomfort was all too apparent.

The assistant felt it his professional duty to point out the folly of buying an eight. 'Sir,' he began, 'I really do think...'

But the customer interrupted him. 'Listen,' he said: 'My wife's just run off with the guy next door, my daughter is living in a squat with a bunch of hippies and my son is a convicted armed robber who has never done an honest day's work in his life. The only pleasure I have left is to come home at night and take off my shoes!'

'Last year for Christmas, I got a humidifier and a dehumidifier. I thought I'd put them in the same room and let them fight it out.'
STEVEN WRIGHT

A young man decided to buy his girlfriend a bracelet for Christmas. The jeweller asked him: 'Would you like your girlfriend's name engraved on it?'

'No,' said the young man after a moment's thought. 'I would like you to engrave the words "To my one and only love".'

'How very romantic,' smiled the jeweller.

'Not really," said the young man. 'This way, if I break up with her, I can use the bracelet again.'

Why was one of the supermarket checkouts worried when the store's sticker gun went out of control?

~

She found there was a price on her head.

On Christmas Eve, a married couple were doing the last-minute supermarket shop for essentials. Suddenly a husband spotted a crate of Budweiser and put it in the shopping trolley.

'What do you think you're doing?' asked the wife. 'They're not essential. We've got plenty of drink at home.'

'They're on offer,' he explained. 'Only £25 for twelve cans.'

'Put them back,' she demanded. 'We can't afford them.'

A few aisles later, she picked up a £50 jar of face cream and put it in the trolley.

'What's going on?' asked the husband indignantly. 'That's not essential.'

'It's my face cream,' she protested. 'It makes me look beautiful.'

'So do twelve cans of Bud,' he said, 'and they're half the price!'

While doing her Christmas shopping, a woman lost her purse in a busy store. It was picked up by an honest little boy and returned to her. When she looked in her purse, she said: 'Hmmm, that's odd. When I lost my purse there was a £20 note. Now there are twenty £1 coins.'

'That's right,' said the boy. 'The last time I found a lady's purse, she didn't have any change for a reward.'

A wife asked her husband to buy organic vege-tables for the Christmas dinner. He went to the supermarket but couldn't be sure whether the vegetables he had picked up were organic, so he asked an elderly male employee for help.

'These vegetables are for my wife. Have they been sprayed with poisonous chemicals?'

'No,' replied the old man. 'You'll have to do that yourself.'

A woman decided to buy her husband some underwear for Christmas. There were three men standing ahead of her in the queue.

The first man said to the sales assistant: 'Two pairs of briefs, please.'

The sales assistant looked at him in disbelief. 'Only two pairs?'

'Yes,' explained the man. 'I wear one pair while the other is in the wash.'

The assistant rang the sale through with barely concealed disgust.

The second man said: 'Five pairs of briefs, please.' 'Only five?' queried the assistant. 'Yes, I wear one pair every day of the week and go commando at the weekend.'

'Well,' said the assistant, shaking his head, 'at least you're better than the last guy.'

Then the third man approached the counter. 'Twelve pairs of briefs.'

The sales assistant smiled: 'At last,' he said. 'A man who knows about hygiene! You must be really clean, sir.'

'I try,' said the customer. 'Now let me just check I've counted right. August, September, October, November . . .'

On the day after Boxing Day, a man went into a shop and said: 'I'd like to return a defective boomerang that I was given as a Christmas present.'

'OK,' said the sales assistant, 'where is it?'

The man said: 'I have no idea.'

> *'My wife is a compulsive shopper. She would buy anything marked down. Once she came home with an escalator.'*
> HENNY YOUNGMAN

A mother was doing her Christmas supermarket shop with a three-year-old girl in her trolley. As they passed the chocolate section, the little girl asked for some chocolate, but the mother said 'No'. The child immediately began to whine, and the mother said quietly: 'Now, Emma, we've only got two more aisles to go. Don't get upset. It won't be long now.'

Soon they arrived at the cookie section, and the child started to beg for some. When told that she couldn't have any, she burst into tears. The mother said quietly: 'No tears, Emma. We've only got one aisle to go. We'll soon be at the checkout.'

When they reached the checkout, the little girl threw a full-blown tantrum when she realized that they hadn't bought her favourite cakes. She screamed the place down and kicked out at her mother. Quietly but firmly, the mother said: 'Emma, we'll be through this checkout in a couple of minutes and then you can go home and have a nice lie-down.'

A man who had witnessed all this caught up with them in the parking lot and praised the mother's approach. He told her: 'I couldn't help but notice how incredibly patient you were in there with little Emma.'

The mother replied: 'Thank you, but I'm Emma. My little girl's name is Sophie.'

It was Christmas and the judge was in a merry mood as he asked the prisoner: 'What are you charged with?'

'Doing my Christmas shopping early,' replied the defendant.

'That's not an offence,' said the judge. 'How early were you doing this shopping?'

'Before the store opened.'

It was the afternoon of Christmas Eve and a man suddenly remembered that he had forgotten to buy the turkey. Without saying a word, he jumped in his car and drove to the shops in record time, arriving just as the butcher was preparing to close for the holiday period.

'Please let me in,' he begged. 'I forgot to buy a turkey for tomorrow. My wife will kill me if I don't come home with one.'

'OK,' said the butcher, happy to make a last-minute sale. 'Let me see what I have left.'

He went to the freezer, but there was only one scrawny turkey left. He brought it out to show the man.

'That one's too skinny,' he said. 'What else have you got?'

The butcher took the bird back to the freezer, and waited a few minutes before bringing the same turkey out again for the man to inspect.

'What about this one?' said the butcher.

'No, that one doesn't look any better,' said the man. 'I'll tell you what: you'd better give me both of them.'

A man was out Christmas shopping when he saw an old lady drop her purse in the High Street outside McDonald's. Before he had the chance to tap her on the shoulder, she boarded a bus. So he sprinted after her and hopped on the bus just as the doors were about to close. Pursuing her to the back of the bus as it pulled away, he said breathlessly: 'You dropped your purse in the street outside McDonald's.'

'Oh, thank you so much, young man,' she said, holding out her hand in expectation. 'Where is it?'

'I just told you,' he said. 'In the street outside McDonald's.'

The department store was so busy on the run-up to Christmas that a man lost his wife somewhere between menswear and bedding. Spotting a pretty girl, he went over to her and said: 'I've lost my wife. Do you mind if I talk to you?'

'Why?' she asked.

'Because every time I talk to a pretty girl, my wife appears out of nowhere!'

'I wrapped my Christmas presents early this year, but I realized I used the wrong wrapping paper. The paper I used said "Happy Birthday". I didn't want to waste it, so I just wrote "Jesus" on it.'
DEMETRI MARTIN

An elderly couple drove to the nearest mall to do their Christmas shopping, after which they stopped for a bite to eat at a restaurant. They were nearly home when the wife suddenly remembered that she had left her glasses at the restaurant.

Annoyed at the prospect of having to drive ten miles back to fetch them, the husband moaned: 'How could you be so forgetful? Sometimes I think you have the memory span of a goldfish! What a waste of an afternoon!'

He was still complaining when they pulled up once more outside the restaurant. As his wife got out of the car, he leaned across and grumbled: 'While you're in there, you may as well get my hat, too.'

Two weeks before Christmas, a woman told her husband: 'I had a lovely dream last night that you were in a jewellery store buying me a diamond ring.'

'That's funny,' said the husband. 'I had the same dream and I saw your dad paying the bill.'

A man went to the perfume counter of a large department store and said he would like a bottle of Chanel No 5, gift wrapped for his wife's Christmas present.

'A little surprise, is it?' asked the sales assistant.

'Yes,' said the man. 'She's expecting a Caribbean cruise!'

Hoping that he was going to get lucky at Christmas, a man went into a large drugstore on Christmas Eve to buy a packet of condoms.

'What size?' asked the sales assistant.

'I don't know,' said the man.

'Go and see Tracey in aisle five,' said the assistant.

So he went to see Tracey who grabbed him by the crotch and yelled out: 'Medium!' Disappointed, the man hurried over to pay and quickly left.

A few minutes later, another man came in to buy condoms. As he did not know what size he needed, he too was sent to see Tracey in aisle five. Tracey immediately grabbed him by the crotch and shouted: 'Large!' Brimming with confidence, he swaggered over to the checkout, paid and left.

Shortly afterwards, a sixteen-year-old schoolboy came in to buy condoms.

'What size?' asked the assistant.

'I don't know,' said the boy. 'I've never done it before.'

The assistant sent him over to Tracey.

A minute later, Tracey called out: 'Cleanup in aisle five!'

A couple went Christmas shopping with their three young children. After hours of trailing around toyshops and hearing their kids ask for every item on the shelves, they were totally fed up.

Weighed down with bags, they squeezed into the crowded lift to take them up to the car park. The husband sighed aloud to nobody in particular: 'Whoever started this whole Christmas thing should be arrested and strung up!'

A voice from the back of the lift replied quietly: 'Don't worry, sir, I believe they crucified him.'

HOW LOVELY TO SEE YOU

Hearing that his wife's sister was coming to spend Christmas with them, a man took his dog to the vet and asked the vet to cut off the animal's tail. Before agreeing to perform the procedure, the vet wanted to know the reason for such drastic action.

'Because', said the man, 'my sister-in-law is arriving tomorrow, and I don't want anything to make her think she's welcome.'

When his grandma arrived for Christmas, a little boy greeted her with a big hug. 'I'm so happy you've come, Grandma. Now maybe Daddy will do the trick he has been promising us.'

'What trick is that?' she asked.

'Well,' said the little boy excitedly. 'I heard him telling Mommy that he would climb the walls if you came to visit us again this year.'

An elderly man had invited his grandson and his partner to come to his apartment on Christmas morning. Giving directions, he said: 'I live at No. 421. On the panel at the front door, use your elbow to push button 421 and I will buzz you in. Come inside and the lift is on the right. Get in the lift and, with your elbow, push fourth floor. When you get out at the fourth floor, turn right and I'm just down the corridor. With your elbow, press my doorbell. Is that all clear?'

'Sure,' said the grandson. 'That sounds easy but why do I have to hit all these buttons with my elbow?'

'Well, you're not coming empty-handed, are you?'

Paul was thirty-four years old and still single. One day a friend asked him: 'Why aren't you married yet? Can't you find the right girl?'

Paul replied: 'Actually, I've found two or three girls who I would have liked to have settled down with but, whenever I take them home to meet my parents, my mother doesn't like them.'

'Perhaps,' said the friend, 'what you need to do is find a girl who is just like your mother.'

A few months later, the two met up again. 'Did you follow my advice?' asked the friend. 'Did you find a girl who's just like your mother?'

'I did,' said Paul glumly. 'I found a girl who is exactly like my mother and I took her to meet my parents at Christmas. And you were right. My mother liked her very much.'

'So what's the problem?'

'My father doesn't like her.'

'You can return all the Christmas gifts you want, but you will never get back the time spent with your relatives.'
ANDY BOROWITZ

A teenage boy was bringing his first girlfriend to Christmas dinner at his parents' house. He had only known her for a week and so was surprised when she accepted the invitation. He told his father that because she was quite shy he was worried that she might feel intimidated among so many strangers.

'What can I talk to her about to make sure the conversation flows?' he asked.

'Well,' said the father, 'there are three subjects that never fail – food, family and philosophy.'

'Thanks, Dad, I'll remember that,' said the boy.

On Christmas Day, the girl nervously sat down next to the boy at the family dinner table. Soon everyone else was laughing and joking but the girl, as he had feared, sat there silently and was in danger of being left out. So, eager to engage her in conversation, he remembered his father's advice about food, family and philosophy and asked her: 'Do you like spinach?'

'No,' she said. And the silence returned.

After a few uncomfortable moments, he thought of the second item on his father's go-to list and asked: 'Do you have any brothers?'

'No,' said the girl again. And the silence returned.

With a desperate last throw of the dice, the boy decided to ask her something philosophical in keeping with his father's third suggestion. So he asked her: 'If you had a brother, would he like spinach?'

A man was watching TV with his wife and mother-in-law on Christmas evening when the latter suddenly declared: 'I've decided that I want to be cremated.'

'OK,' said the man. 'I'll get your coat.'

A man was dismayed because his wife had insisted that her grumpy old father come to spend Christmas with them. The two men had never got on, chiefly because the father rarely wasted an opportunity to belittle his son-in-law. After two awkward days, the son-in-law was eagerly looking forward to the time when his nemesis would be heading home.

On the third morning, he went into the bedroom where his wife was tidying up and told her: 'Your father tripped over some of Michael's Lego bricks fifteen minutes ago, fell awkwardly and looks to be in some pain.'

'Fifteen minutes ago?!' she screamed. 'Why are you only telling me about this now?'

'Because I've only just stopped laughing.'

After experiencing a fraught morning, a woman answered the phone and was relieved to hear a friendly voice on the other end. 'Oh, Mother,' she sobbed, 'I've had a terrible morning. First, I sprained my ankle, so I haven't been able to go shopping. The refrigerator has broken, the washing machine flooded the kitchen and I haven't been able to do any Christmas preparations. And we've got friends coming round tonight for dinner. What am I going to do?'

'Now, don't you worry about a thing. I'll be over in half an hour. I'll do the shopping, clean up the house and cook your dinner. I'll call a repairman for the fridge and the washing machine, I'll do everything. And I'll call Simon at work to tell him he ought to come home and help.'

'Simon? Who's Simon?'

'Simon – your husband! This is 469 2813, isn't it?'

'No, this is 469 2814.'

'Oh.'

'Does this mean you're not coming over?!'

A senior couple were enjoying Christmas at their son's house 200 miles away when the woman suddenly sat bolt upright in her fireside chair and exclaimed: 'Oh, no! I've just remembered I left the oven on at home!'

'Don't worry,' said her husband reassuringly. 'The house won't burn down. I've just remembered I left the bath running!'

Neil had invited his elderly parents to spend Christmas with him. While Neil and his father were sitting around the fire, the father began talking about a delightful restaurant that he and Neil's mother had visited recently.

'What was the name of the restaurant?' asked Neil.

'I'm damned if I can remember,' replied the father. 'Help me here. What's the name of that beautiful flower? It smells exquisite and is thorny.'

'A rose?' suggested Neil.

'That's it!' exclaimed his father who then turned around and called out: 'Hey, Rose, what was the name of that restaurant we went to last week?'

What's the difference between
in-laws and outlaws?

~

Outlaws are wanted.

'Darling,' said a husband to his wife, 'I've invited a friend over for Christmas.'

'What?!' she exclaimed. 'Are you crazy? The house is a mess, the kids are feral, I haven't got enough food in and I really can't be bothered to cook anything special, Christmas or not.'

'I know all that.'

'So why did you invite him?'

'Because the poor fool's thinking about getting married.'

Grandma phoned out of the blue to say she would be arriving at her daughter's home for Christmas, a day earlier than expected. In fact, she said, she would be there in about an hour.

When she arrived, she was surprised and delighted to see her young grandson rush out to greet her with the words: 'Now that you're here, Grandma, we have everything!'

'Whatever do you mean?' asked Grandma.

'Well, when you called,' said the boy, 'I heard my Dad say, "That's all we need."'

Announcing that she was bringing her new boyfriend to visit on Boxing Day, a young woman told her mother excitedly: 'I've found a man just like Dad!'

'What do you expect from me?' asked the mother. 'Sympathy?'

Two old men went to visit their friend George at Christmas. The nostalgic conversation flowed pleasantly for a while until George suddenly stood up and said: 'How silly of me! I haven't even offered you coffee.' So he got up and made some coffee.

Forty-five minutes later, George suddenly stood up again and said: 'How silly of me! I haven't even offered you coffee.' And off he went to the kitchen to make some.

An hour later, he said and did the same thing for a third time.

A couple of hours later, the two left. As the door closed behind them, one old man turned to the other and said: 'Don't you think George was acting odd? All that time we were there and he never even offered us coffee!'

'What?!' said the other. 'You've been to see George, and you didn't invite me!'

One Christmas, a daughter announced her sudden engagement.

Her shocked father asked: 'Does this fellow have any money?'

The daughter shook her head in despair. 'Honestly, Daddy,' she said, 'you men are all the same.'

'What do you mean?' asked her father.

'Well,' she replied, 'that's exactly what he asked me about you.'

A woman, her husband and her parents all went out to a busy restaurant for Christmas dinner. The conversation was stilted for the most part because the woman's father was not the easiest person in the world to get along with. After a couple of minutes of silence, the husband, trying to make small talk, remarked: 'The service here is a bit slow today.'

'Tell me something I don't know!' barked the father dismissively.

A lengthy period of silence followed until the husband, in another attempt to break the ice, ventured: 'At least it's not snowing outside. So far this winter has been incredibly mild.'

'Tell me something I don't know!' snapped the father. And the silence returned.

As they finished their main courses, the husband said innocently: 'My beef dish was delicious. You really can't beat good beef.'

'Tell me something I don't know!' said the father with a sneer. Silence followed.

When it was time to pay the bill, the husband said: 'It looks as if it's going to be tough year for the economy.'

'Tell me something I don't know!' roared the father.

Finally releasing his pent-up irritation, the husband responded: 'Your daughter's heavily into BDSM.'

After several months of dating, Maisie finally introduced her boyfriend, Josh, to her parents at Christmas.

They wasted little time in exploring his family background. 'What does your father do, Josh?' they asked.

'He's a magician,' replied Josh.

'Oh! How wonderful!' they exclaimed. 'What's his best trick?'

'He saws people in half,' said Josh.

'How incredible!' they gushed in perfect unison. 'And do you have any brothers or sisters?'

'Yes,' he said. 'One half brother and two half sisters.'

Eunice was travelling by train to see her family at Christmas. When another lady sat in the seat next to her, Eunice, being a friendly sort, quickly struck up a conversation.

'I'm always so excited about Christmas,' she told the stranger, 'because my grandson was born on Christmas Eve. He'll be four this year. It doesn't seem possible. They grow up so quickly. It seems like only yesterday that he was still in diapers playing with his teddy bear. I can't wait to see him again.

'He's the most adorable little boy. And he's so clever. Everyone says his handwriting and speech are very advanced for his age. He's already started learning French and Spanish. I'm sure he's going to leave his mark in this world, maybe as a doctor or a lawyer, but I just know he'll be outstanding in whatever profession he chooses.

'Wait, I'm sure I have a photo of him in my handbag. Yes, here's one. Look at him. Isn't he just the cutest little boy, with his little button nose and those dimples? And that lovely blond hair. Oh, I could just eat him! He's so perfect. And he has a wonderful singing voice, the voice of an angel. He's very musical, you know. He's starting piano lessons next year.

'And when he talks to me on the phone and says, "Hi, Grandma," I must say I get very emotional. I'm just so very proud of him . . . Oh, but I'm so sorry. Here I am just talking and talking without letting you get a word in edgeways! So tell me, what do *you* think about my grandson?'

When a family's elderly relatives descended on the house for Christmas, the youngest boy made little attempt to disguise his disappointment. Eventually he turned to one of them and said: 'Aunt Hermione, you're ugly!'

His father overheard the remark and was appalled. He took the boy to one side and gave him a good telling-off before ordering him to go back and say sorry to Aunt Hermione.

Suitably chastened, the boy went over and said: 'Aunt Hermione, I'm sorry you're ugly.'

The whole family had gone to the wife's parents' house on Christmas afternoon, but sadly her elderly father, who was notorious for being careful with money, was taken seriously ill in the evening. As he lay on his deathbed determined to spend his last few hours in his own room, he gently raised his head off the pillow and, summoning what little remaining strength he had, asked softly: 'Is my beloved wife Clara here?'

'Yes, I am here,' she replied.

The old man went on: 'Are my two children here, my wonderful children?'

'Yes, Dad,' they replied. 'We are both here.'

'And are my three delightful grandchildren here?'

'Yes, we are here, Grandpa,' they said.

'So,' said the old man, flopping his head back down onto the pillow, 'if everyone is here, why is the light on in the kitchen?'

An old man was flying to Seattle to spend Christmas with his daughter, but after encountering some turbulence the landing was especially bumpy. When it was time to disembark, the cabin crew stood at the door of the airplane while the passengers exited.

The crew thanked each person in turn for flying with the airline, and wished them a safe onward journey. The old man was the last to leave. Still unnerved by the landing, he quietly asked the flight attendant: 'Do you mind if I ask you a question, young lady?'

'Sure,' replied the flight attendant.

'Did we land or were we shot down?'

At Christmas, a young man was invited to his girlfriend's house for the first time. Left alone in the lounge for a minute, he spotted a small, decorative vase on the sideboard and picked it up. Just then the girl walked in.

'What's this?' he asked, tilting the vase to inspect the base.

'My father's ashes are in there,' she said.

'Oh, my God!' he exclaimed, quickly putting it back in its place on the sideboard. 'I'm so sorry. I had no idea ...'

'Yes,' she continued, 'he's too lazy to go to the kitchen and get an ashtray.'

On Christmas Eve, Bob called his son in New York and said: 'Raymond, I'm divorcing your mother.'

'But you can't,' said Raymond. 'You've been married forty-eight years.'

'I'm sorry,' said Bob, 'but I don't want to discuss it. My mind's made up. I just thought I ought to let you know.'

'Can I talk to Mom?' asked Raymond.

'No, you can't talk to your mother because I haven't told her yet. But I'm seeing a lawyer in three days' time – the day after Boxing Day.'

Raymond couldn't believe what he was hearing. 'Listen, Dad, don't do anything hasty. I'll catch the first flight down to Florida. I'll be with you as soon as I can. So can we at least talk about this as a family before you start filing for divorce?'

'All right,' said Bob. 'I'll listen to what you have to say. Will you call your sister in New Jersey and break the news to her? I can't bear to talk about it any longer.'

Half an hour later, Bob received a phone call from his daughter in New Jersey who said that she and her brother had got tickets, and they and the children would be arriving in Florida the next day. She made him promise not to do anything rash. Bob promised, and put down the phone. Then he turned to his wife and said: 'Well, it worked this time, but what are we going to do to get them to come down next Christmas?'

Fred and Mildred, a couple in their seventies, went to visit their daughter and son-in-law at their brand new house on Christmas Day. After an excellent dinner, Fred went to the bathroom and, on his return, while the rest of the family were in the kitchen doing the washing-up, started raving to his wife about the magnificent golden toilet bowl. 'I've never seen one like it, Mildred,' he told her excitedly. 'It's pure gold. It's incredible.'

Before Mildred had a chance to see it for herself, it was time for them to leave but, on the way home, Fred kept going on about the superb golden toilet bowl in his daughter's new house. When they arrived home, he was still so excited that he immediately went next door to his friend George's house, and told him all about the golden toilet bowl.

'You have to see it,' said Fred. 'Go round there now. My daughter and son-in-law won't mind. They don't go to bed until late. Just tell them I sent you.'

So George drove to Fred's daughter's house. When the daughter answered the door, George explained the reason for his visit. 'Your father told me about the magnificent golden toilet bowl in your house and said I just had to see it for myself. You know what he's like!'

Hearing this, the daughter turned back into the house and called out: 'Terry, I know who crapped in your tuba!'

HOW LOVELY TO SEE YOU

'My mother-in-law has come round to our
house at Christmas seven years in a row.
This year we're having a change.
We're going to let her in.'
LES DAWSON

Reading a letter that had just arrived in the post, a woman turned to look suspiciously at her husband. 'Dennis, mother says she isn't accepting our invitation to come and stay for Christmas because it appears that we don't want her here. What does she mean? I told you to write and say that she was to come at her convenience. You did write, didn't you?'

'Er, yes,' said the husband hesitantly. 'But I couldn't spell "convenience" so I put "risk".'

A man was flying to Spain to see his family at Christmas. The seat next to him on the plane was occupied by a smartly dressed woman in her fifties. Suddenly the woman sneezed, took out a tissue, wiped her nose and then visibly shuddered for about ten seconds.

The man resumed reading his book, but a few minutes later she sneezed again, produced a tissue, wiped her nose and shuddered for about fifteen seconds.

He assumed she must have a heavy cold but was mystified by the shuddering. Worried that it might be contagious, he was trying to edge away from her when she sneezed again, took out a tissue and wiped her nose. This time her entire body shuddered for at least twenty seconds.

Unable to suppress his curiosity about the shuddering any longer, he turned to her and said: 'I couldn't help noticing that you've sneezed three times, wiped your nose on a tissue and then shuddered violently. Are you OK?'

'I'm so sorry if I am disturbing you,' said the woman. 'You see I have a very rare medical condition. Whenever I sneeze I have an orgasm.'

'That's certainly not a condition I've ever heard of,' said the man, slightly embarrassed by her revelation. 'Are you taking anything for it?'

'Yes,' she said. 'Pepper.'

Before all the aunts and uncles arrived on Christmas Day, a small boy asked his father: 'How were people born?'

The father said: 'Well, Adam and Eve made babies, then their babies became adults and they made babies, too. And it went on from there.'

The boy was not entirely convinced by the answer, so a few minutes later he asked his mother the same question.

She told him: 'We were monkeys, and then we evolved to become what we are now.'

The boy ran back to his father and said: 'Dad, you got it wrong! We came from monkeys!'

'No,' said the father, 'your mum was talking about her side of the family.'

A girl invited her boyfriend to come to her parents' house for Christmas dinner. She realized it was a daunting prospect, but as an inducement she said that after the dinner she wanted to go out with him and lose her virginity.

To prepare for this, the boy, who was also a virgin, went to a pharmacist to buy a packet of condoms. The pharmacist was extremely helpful and told him everything he wanted to know about sex. Finally, he asked the boy whether he wanted a three-pack, a six-pack or a family pack.

'I think I'd better take a family pack,' said the boy, 'because I reckon I'm going to be busy over the next few nights.'

The boy arrived as arranged for Christmas dinner and was greeted at the front door by his girlfriend. She then showed him into the dining room where her parents were already seated at the table. Sitting down, the boy quickly offered to say grace and bowed his head. After fifteen minutes, his head was still down.

His girlfriend leaned over and said: 'I had no idea you were so religious.'

The boy whispered back: 'And I had no idea your father was a pharmacist.'

Following yet another Christmas argument with his wife, a wealthy man decided to change his will so that she would inherit everything on condition that she remarried within three months of his death.

'Why do you want that to happen?' asked his lawyer.

'Because I want *someone* to be sorry I died.'

An elderly woman was travelling by Greyhound bus from St Louis to spend Christmas with her family. The bus had barely left St Louis when the woman asked the driver: 'Are we at Kansas City yet?'

'No,' said the driver. 'I'll let you know when we are.'

Fifteen minutes later, she asked him again: 'Are we at Kansas City yet?'

'No,' he answered curtly. 'Like I say, I'll let you know when we are.'

She kept this up for the next four and a half hours. Every fifteen minutes or so, she would ask the driver whether they had arrived yet at Kansas

City and each time he would tell her 'No'. With each interruption, he could feel his heart racing and throbbing uncontrollably and the tension building up inside his body, but he still did his utmost to remain professional and courteous. Finally, with his nerves by now in tatters, they pulled into Kansas City bus station and, breathing a deep sigh of relief, he called out: 'OK, madam, this is Kansas City. Off you get.'

'Oh no, driver,' she said, 'I'm going all the way to Denver. It's just that my daughter told me that when we reached Kansas City I should take my blood pressure tablet.'

A young man – an only child – had finally got engaged, but was apprehensive about bringing his fiancée to meet his parents at Christmas because his mother was notoriously judgmental. Eventually he was persuaded to do so but told his mother: 'I'm going to bring home three girls and I want you to guess which one is my fiancée.'

Sure enough the next day he arrived with three

girls in tow. Addressing his mother, he said: 'Now which one do you think is my fiancée?'

'That one,' she said instantly, pointing to the girl on the right.

'How on earth did you know that?' he said incredulously.

'Because I don't like her,' the mother replied.

A family had invited half a dozen relatives for Christmas dinner. At the table, the mother turned to her six-year-old daughter and said: 'Darling, would you like to say the blessing?'

'I wouldn't know what to say,' replied the little girl shyly.

'Just say what you hear Daddy say,' suggested the mother.

The little girl took a deep breath, bowed her head and solemnly said: 'Dear Lord, why on earth did we invite all these people to dinner?'

IT'S THE THOUGHT
THAT COUNTS

A couple had two five-year-old children, Ben and Claire, who, despite being twins, had entirely different attitudes to life. Ben was a born pessimist while Claire was an eternal optimist. The marked contrast caused their parents considerable concern, especially when it came to buying presents.

So one year the parents decided to consult a child psychiatrist about what to buy their children for Christmas. The psychiatrist recommended spending as much as they could afford on Ben the pessimist, but said that Claire the optimist would probably be happy with anything. 'Why not get a pile of manure and wrap that up for Claire?' he suggested. 'I'm sure she'll be fine with that.'

The parents took the psychiatrist's advice and spent a lot of money on presents for Ben and wrapped a heap of manure for Claire.

On Christmas morning, the children were opening their presents. 'What has Santa Claus bought you?' they asked Ben.

Ben answered gloomily: 'A bike, but I'll probably get run over while riding it; football boots, but I'll probably break my leg while playing; and an electric train set, but I'll probably electrocute myself.'

Dismayed at his response, they quickly turned to Claire. 'And what has Santa Claus bought you, Claire?' they asked.

'I think I got a pony,' said Claire, up to her elbows in manure. 'But I haven't been able to find him yet!'

*'I love Christmas. I receive a lot of wonderful
presents I can't wait to exchange.'*
HENNY YOUNGMAN

A couple were so poor that, no matter how they juggled their finances, they realized they simply could not afford to buy their son a Christmas present.

'We have to give him something,' said the mother.

'Don't worry,' said the father. 'I'll be creative.'

Sure enough, on Christmas morning the boy woke to find a neatly wrapped parcel at the foot of his bed. But when he undid the wrapping, he found just an empty shoe box.

'What's this?' he asked tearfully.

His father explained: 'It's an Action Man deserter.'

A man stopped off at a toyshop to buy a cricket bat for his son for Christmas. At the cash desk, the clerk asked: 'Cash or card?'

'Cash,' snapped the customer, before apologizing. 'I'm sorry, but I've just spent the entire afternoon at the car pound after my van was towed away. It's been so frustrating.'

The clerk said: 'Shall I giftwrap the bat or are you going back there?'

Having recently passed his driving test, a young man asked his clergyman father whether he could have a car for Christmas even though it was still seven months away. His father gave the matter careful thought before replying: 'I'll tell you what I'll do. If you get good grades in your exams, study your Bible and get your hair cut, we may be able to buy you a car for Christmas.'

Three months later, the young man raised the subject again. His father said: 'Your exam grades were excellent and I'm impressed by the way in which you have applied yourself to your Bible studies but I am a little disappointed that you haven't had your hair cut.'

Quick as a flash, the young man said: 'Well, from my Bible studies I've noticed in the illustrations that Moses, John the Baptist, Samson and even Jesus all had long hair.'

'Yes, I'm aware of that,' said his father, 'but did you also notice that they walked everywhere?'

'I bought my wife a mood ring for Christmas,'
a man told his friend. 'When she's in a good
mood, it turns green; when she's in a bad mood,
it leaves a red mark on my chin.'

A week before Christmas, a woman said to her husband: 'I had a dream last night where you gave me the most beautiful diamond necklace. What do you think it means?'

'You'll know in a week's time,' he said with a smile.

The woman could hardly think of anything else for the rest of the week and couldn't wait for Christmas to arrive. On Christmas morning she was the first in the house to rise – even ahead of the children – and excitedly scanned the bedroom for signs of a present. There, on the bedside table, sat a small package. It was a gift from her husband. Ripping the festive wrapping paper off frenziedly, she opened it to find a book titled *The Meaning of Dreams*.

A young boy was heard praying loudly a week before Christmas. 'Dear God, I pray that I will get a video game for Christmas.'

'Why are you shouting?' asked his mother. 'God isn't deaf.'

'I know,' said the boy, 'but Granny is.

'When it comes to Christmas presents, it's not the thought that counts, it's the receipt.'
MILES KINGTON

Knowing that her husband wanted to try paint-balling in the New Year, a wife decided to buy him a pair of camouflage pants for Christmas. So she went to an army surplus store and asked if they had any camouflage pants.

'Yes, we do,' said the sales assistant, 'but we can't find them!'

A few days before Christmas, a boy told his father: 'Dad, you can delete the train set from my Christmas wish list.'

'Why's that?' asked the father, concerned.

'Because yesterday I found one in the cupboard under the stairs.'

For Christmas, a woman bought her husband a lie detector robot that slapped people whenever they told a lie. He decided to test it on his son.

'When you go round to Ben's house, what do you usually do?' asked the father.

'Oh, nothing much,' said the son.

The robot slapped the son.

'Okay, we watch DVDs.'

'What sort?' asked the father.

'Things like Harry Potter.'

The robot slapped the son again.

'OK, we watch porn,' admitted the son.

The father exploded: 'When I was your age I didn't even know what porn was!'

The robot slapped the father.

'Ha! ha!' laughed the mother. 'It's easy to see he's your son!'

The robot slapped the mother.

Three brothers – Luke, Jonny and Seth – decided to buy special Christmas presents for their beloved grandfather.

Luke sent him a new set of golf clubs 'because Grandpa has always loved a game of golf'.

Jonny sent him a new smartphone 'so Grandpa can keep in contact with his friends'.

Seth came up with an ingenious idea. 'You

know how Grandpa hates to read, but likes to be read to? Well, I've decided to send him a parrot that I've seen for sale online. This parrot is specially trained to read from a book. It's really expensive – over £1,800 – but I reckon Grandpa is worth it.'

A week after Christmas, the three brothers each received letters from their grandfather.

Luke's letter read: 'I've given up playing golf, because my knees are wrecked. But thank you for the kind thought, Luke.'

Jonny's letter read: 'I can't be doing with all this new technology, and lovely though the phone is, I can't see myself ever using it. But thank you for the kind thought, Jonny.'

Seth's letter read: 'Seth, you've always been my favourite grandson, so I knew I could rely on you to come up with the perfect Christmas gift. That chicken you sent was delicious.'

Two friends were talking about the Christmas presents they had bought and received. One said: 'I bought my son a BB gun.'

'And what did he get you?' asked the other.

'A sweater with a bullseye on the back.'

A man decided to surprise his girlfriend by paying her an unexpected visit at Christmas. When she answered the door, she was shocked to see him standing there. 'What are you doing?' she asked.

'And why aren't you wearing a shirt? And ... you're covered in baby oil.'

'Well,' he smiled, 'you know how you always say I never glisten . . .?'

'Listen. You never LISTEN.'

'Oh.'

*Can you remember that awkward moment
when you were about five years old and realized
that Santa Claus was using the same wrapping
paper as your parents?*

A two-year-old girl was given a tea set for Christmas. It quickly became one of her favourite toys, and when her mother went away for a few days to care for a sick relative, the toddler loved nothing more than to take her father a cup of tea, which was really just water, while he was watching TV.

He sipped each 'cup of tea' he was brought and always told his daughter how wonderful it tasted.

When the mother returned home, her husband couldn't wait to show her how well their little princess had been looking after him. On cue, the girl took him his 'cup of tea' and he sipped it before bestowing generous praise on its quality.

The mother watched him drink it and then said to him: 'Did it ever occur to you that the only place a toddler can reach to get water is . . . the toilet?'

As a Christmas gift to his new son-in-law, a successful businessman gave him a half share of the firm. 'From now on,' said the businessman, 'we're equal partners. All you have to do is go down to the factory each day and learn the ropes.'

'I couldn't do that,' said the son-in-law. 'I hate factories. They're such noisy places.'

'That's not a problem,' said the businessman, still exuding festive bonhomie. 'We'll put you in the office instead. You can oversee the administrative side of things.'

'No way!' said the son-in-law. 'I don't want to be stuck behind a desk all day.'

Unsurprisingly, the businessman was becoming irritated by this display of ingratitude and said: 'Now look here. I've just made you half-owner of a thriving company. First, I offer you a senior management position in the factory, but you don't want it. Then I offer you a senior management position in the office, but you don't want that either. What am I going to do with you?'

The son-in-law replied: 'You could always buy me out.'

A man opened a Christmas card and found that it was full of rice.

'What's that?' asked his wife.

'It's from my Uncle Ben.'

'Ever wonder what people got Jesus for Christmas? It's like, "Oh, great, socks. You know I'm dying for your sins, right? Yeah, but thanks for the socks! They'll go great with my sandals. What am I, German?"'

JIM GAFFIGAN

When his young daughter said she would like a Barbie doll for Christmas, a man visited the local toyshop and asked to see the range of Barbie dolls.

The sales girl said: 'We have Barbie Goes to the Gym at £20, Barbie Goes to the Ball at £20, Barbie Goes Shopping at £20, Barbie Goes Clubbing at £20 and Divorced Barbie at £200.'

The man was puzzled. 'Why are the others all £20 and yet Divorced Barbie costs £200?'

'Because,' replied the sales girl, 'divorced Barbie comes with Ken's house, Ken's furniture, Ken's car and Ken's boat.'

A man bought his wife a lovely looking diamond ring for Christmas.

A friend said: 'I thought she wanted one of those 4 x 4 vehicles?'

'She did,' said the husband. 'But where on earth was I going to find a fake jeep?'

Two six-year-old girls were talking during school lunch in the run-up to Christmas.

'What are you hoping to get for Christmas?' said one.

'A Tampax,' said the other.

'What's that?'

'I don't know, but it says if you get one you can do everything. Go to the gym, swim, ride a bike ... even ride a horse!'

Chatting to his neighbour about their respective Christmases, a man said: 'Unfortunately, the sweater my kids bought me kept picking up static electricity.'

'That's a shame,' said the neighbour. 'What did you do?'

'Well, luckily I took it back and exchanged it for another one – free of charge.'

A man arrived home on Christmas Eve with a lovely bunch of flowers for his wife.

Suspecting an ulterior motive behind this uncharacteristically romantic gesture, she said: 'I guess that means I'll have to spread my legs now?'

'Why?' he said. 'Don't we have a vase?'

'He was a great dad. Every year he got so mad when Santa didn't bring me presents.'
HOMER SIMPSON, *THE SIMPSONS*

Struggling to think of something different to buy his partner's mother for Christmas, Harry thought it might be a nice idea to get her a large burial plot in an exclusive cemetery, a gift that certainly didn't come cheap. In fact, it was so expensive that the following year he didn't buy her anything, which prompted her to complain bitterly.

'I don't know what you're complaining about,' he said. 'You still haven't used the present I bought you last year.'

A woman was showing a friend the new designer coat that her husband had bought her for Christmas.

'I've seen that coat online,' said the friend. 'It costs a fortune. That's very generous of him.'

'He had no choice. I caught him kissing the maid.'

'How dreadful!' said the friend sympathetically. 'Did you fire her?'

'Certainly not. I still need the matching hat.'

'What did you buy your mother for Christmas?' asked a neighbour.

'A new refrigerator,' came the reply. 'You should have seen her face light up when she opened it.'

As a surprise Christmas gift a man researched, wrote and printed a book, chronicling his wife's family tree covering a period of more than 600 years. She thought it was a wonderful gesture but was worried what the book might say about the black sheep of the family, her great-grandfather Elias, who had been executed in the electric chair.

'Don't worry,' said the husband, 'I've handled it with the utmost tact.'

She quickly turned to the section covering her great-grandfather and read: 'Elias Hampton occupied a chair of applied electrics at an important government institution. He was attached to his position by the strongest of ties. His death came as a real shock.'

On Christmas morning a Montana police officer on horseback was waiting at a traffic light and, next to him, was a young boy on his brand new bike.

'Nice bike you got there,' said the cop. 'Did Santa bring that to you?'

'Yeah,' said the kid.

'Well, next year,' continued the cop, 'tell Santa to put a tail-light on that bike.' And he proceeded to issue the kid with a $20 bicycle safety violation ticket.

The kid took the ticket but then said to the cop: 'By the way, that's a nice horse you got there. Did Santa bring that to you?'

Humouring the kid, the cop replied: 'Yeah, he sure did.'

'Well,' said the kid, 'next year tell Santa to put the dick underneath the horse instead of on top!'

A woman asked her husband to buy her a twenty-three-piece China tea set for Christmas.

As she opened the package excitedly on Christmas morning, he said: 'Actually, you'll find that you've got a forty-six-piece China tea set.'

'Oh, that's so generous of you!' she squealed, giving him a big hug.

'Not really,' he said. 'I dropped it getting out of the car.'

Two neighbours were chatting over the garden fence. 'What did you buy your wife for Christmas?' asked one.
'A vibrator,' whispered the other. 'And she's done nothing but moan ever since!'

One Christmas, a father decided that he was no longer going to remind his children to send thank you letters because it was about time they started to think for themselves. As a result, the kids' grandfather never received thanks for the Christmas cheques he had sent them.

However, the following Christmas the children, without any encouragement from their father, all made a point of travelling over to their grandfather's house to thank him personally for their cheques.

'That was quite a change in attitude,' said the father quietly to the grandfather. 'Any idea what brought it about?'

'Simple,' said the grandfather. 'This year I didn't sign the cheques.'

*'Christmas sweaters are only acceptable
as a cry for help.'*
Andy Borowitz

When their ten-year-old son began misbehaving at school and getting bad grades, his parents decided that he would have to buck up if he wanted to get anything for Christmas. 'So,' they told him, 'quickly mend your ways or forget the video game console.' On his last day at school before the holiday, they were eager to see his report card.

'I don't have it,' he said, when he arrived home.

'Why not?' asked his father firmly.

'My friend Billy has it.'

'Why has your friend Billy got your school report card?'

'Because,' said the boy sheepishly, 'he wanted to scare his parents.'

'This past Christmas, I told my girlfriend for months in advance that all I wanted was an Xbox. That's it. Beginning and end of list; Xbox. You know what she got me? A homemade frame with a picture of us from our first date together. Which was fine – because I got her an Xbox.'

Anthony Jeselnik

A wife told her notoriously mean husband: 'I really need a new dress for Christmas.'

'Why?' he asked. 'What's wrong with the one you've got?'

'Well, it's too long and, besides, the veil keeps getting in my eyes.'

Two friends were chatting in a bar at New Year. One said: 'What did you get your wife for Christmas?'
The other replied: 'A bag and a belt. She wasn't happy, but the Hoover works fine now.'

For Christmas a man bought his wife of forty years a new line of expensive cosmetics that promised to make her look years younger. After carefully applying them over a period of several hours, she said: 'Darling, tell me honestly, what age would you say I am?'

He studied her closely before replying: 'Judging from your skin, twenty-four; your hair, twenty-five; and your figure, twenty-eight.'

'Oh, you silver-tongued flatterer!' she gushed.

'Not so fast,' he said. 'I haven't added them up yet!'

A man bought his wife a diamond necklace for Christmas, but she was unimpressed.

'Why did you buy me such a small diamond?' she complained.

He said: 'I didn't want the glare to hurt your eyes.'

A father asked his young daughter what she would like for Christmas. To his surprise, she said that what she wanted more than anything else was a baby brother. And it so happened that on Christmas Eve her mother came home from hospital carrying a baby boy.

The following year, the father again asked his daughter what she would like for Christmas.

'Well,' she replied, 'if it's not too uncomfortable for Mummy, I'd like a pony.'

A man bought his elderly father a brand new toilet brush as a small gift for Christmas. But, when he went to visit a few weeks later, there was no sign of it in the bathroom.

'Dad, what happened to the loo brush I bought you?'

'I'm sorry, son, but I just couldn't take to it. After all these years, I guess I've got used to toilet paper. That new thing was way too scratchy.'

'Christmas presents: unwrapping proof that the people you love don't know you at all.'
SARA PASCOE

Don and Jim were talking in the pub. 'What did you get your wife for Christmas?' asked Don.

'When I asked her,' replied Jim, 'she said she wanted a new winter coat. So that's what I got her – a winter coat. What about you?'

'Well,' said Don, 'when I asked my wife what

she wanted she said that nothing would make her happier than a 24-carat gold ring. So that's what I got her – nothing.'

Because his wife had complained of feeling lonely while he was out at work all day, a man decided to buy her a parrot for Christmas. So he went along to a pet auction and spotted the ideal bird, a handsome African grey.

The bidding started off at £20 but kept going up and up. The man was desperate not to miss out on the parrot, but no matter how much he bid another bidder was equally determined. Soon the bidding had reached £900. The man knew this was getting out of hand and vowed that £1000 would be his absolute limit. Fortunately, when the bidding reached that total, the rival bidder dropped out. Although the man had paid way more for the bird than intended, the parrot was now his.

As he was paying for it, he said to the auctioneer: 'For all this money, I really hope this parrot can talk.'

'Don't worry, he can talk,' said the auctioneer. 'Who do you think was bidding against you?'

Where is the best place to hide
Christmas presents?

~

In the mouth of a gift horse.

A married couple were debating what to buy her mother for Christmas. 'She told me she would like something electric,' said the wife.

'How about a chair?' suggested the husband.

'Christmases were terrible, not like nowadays
when kids get everything. My sister got a
miniature set of perfumes called "AMPLE". It
was tiny, but even I could see where my dad
had scraped off the "S".'
STEPHEN K. AMOS

The judge glared at the accused: 'So you admit breaking into the women's clothing store?'

'Yes, Your Honour.'

'And why was that?'

'Because my wife wanted a new dress for Christmas.'

The judge looked at his notes. 'But it says here that you broke into the same shop four times – first on 23 December and then three nights in a row – on 27, 28 and 29 December.'

'Yes, Your Honour. She kept making me exchange it.'

'What did you get from Grandma for Christmas?' asked the boy's mother.

'Three socks,' he replied with a shrug of his shoulders.

The mother was mystified by such a strange gift, so when she spoke to Grandma later that day, she asked why she had bought the boy three socks.

Grandma said: 'Because you told me he had grown another foot in the past year.'

A man sat at the bar looking thoroughly depressed. After a while the bartender asked: 'What's wrong?'

The man sighed: 'I'll never understand women. On Christmas morning my wife told me that later on, as her gift to me, I could do with her whatever I wanted.'

'Wow!' said the bartender. 'Sounds like a great gift! Then why are you so miserable?'

'Well,' said the man. 'I thought about it and sent her home to her mother's. Now she won't even speak to me.'

Two women friends met after dropping their children off at school at the start of the new term. 'What did your husband get you for Christmas?' asked one.

'A skirt and sex,' replied the other. 'Both were too short.'

On Christmas Eve, a man suddenly realized that he hadn't bought a present for his new girlfriend. Short of money, he popped into a department store and headed for the cosmetics counter.

'What perfume would you recommend?' he asked the sales assistant.

Reaching into the glass cabinet behind her, she said: 'This is one of our bestsellers, only £50 a bottle.'

'That's too expensive,' he said. 'What else do you have?'

'Well,' she said, fetching a different brand, 'this perfume is always very popular, and it's only £30 a bottle.'

'Sorry, that's still too much,' he said.

The assistant was becoming annoyed by his meanness but, eager not to lose a sale, she said: 'We do have this one at £10.'

The man shuffled awkwardly. 'What I mean,' he whispered, 'is I'd like to see something real cheap.'

So the sales assistant handed him a mirror.

For Christmas, a wife asked her husband for something that did nought to sixty in five seconds. So he bought her ... bathroom scales.

*'Oh, joy, Christmas Eve! By this time
tomorrow, millions of Americans, knee-deep
in tinsel and wrapping paper, will utter those
heartfelt words: "Is this all I got?"'*
FRASIER CRANE, *CHEERS*

On the day after Christmas, the vicar was looking at the church nativity scene when he noticed that the baby Jesus had gone missing. He thought he might need to report the theft but before he had a chance to do so, he spotted a young boy outside the church. He was pushing a toy plastic train engine and a carriage around the church grounds and inside the carriage was the missing figure of Jesus.

The vicar approached the boy and, gesturing at the figure of Jesus, asked: 'Where did you get your passenger?'

The boy replied: 'I took him from the church.'

'And why did you take him?' asked the vicar.

'Well, about a week before Christmas I prayed to the Lord Jesus. I promised him if he would bring me a train and carriage for Christmas, I would give him a ride around the block in it.'

Leo was given a parrot as a Christmas present. Unfortunately, the parrot's previous owner had taught it to swear, with the result that every other word was an obscenity.

Leo tried everything to improve the bird's behaviour, teaching it nice words, playing it soothing music, but nothing could stem the stream of expletives. And the angrier he became with the parrot, the ruder the parrot's language. Eventually, at the end of his tether and in a moment of desperation, he decided to put the parrot in the freezer for thirty seconds in the hope that the extreme punishment might teach it a lesson.

Sure enough, when Leo opened the freezer door the parrot was a reformed character. Gone were the bad attitude, the squawking and swearing. In its place was a gentle, chastened bird. The freezer treatment had obviously worked better than Leo could have hoped.

As the parrot stepped out of the freezer, it said quietly: 'I am truly sorry if my coarse and unseemly language offended you. I realize now that I was completely out of order, so please accept my sincerest apologies. I can assure you that it will not happen again. I have just one question.'

'What's that?' said Leo.

'Tell me,' said the parrot, 'what did the turkey do?'

Two neighbours were discussing their Christmases. One said: 'I have a cousin who is a keen chef, so I bought her a new top-of-the-range frying pan for Christmas.'

'That's nice,' said the other. 'I have a friend who is visually impaired but he loves to cook, so I bought him a cheese grater for Christmas.'

'Has he used it much for cooking?'

'I'm not sure, but he did say it was the most dangerous book he'd ever read.'

Mark and Jim had season tickets to watch Manchester United. They couldn't help noticing that there was always a spare seat, F12, next to them and they had a friend who was desperate to buy a season ticket, especially if they could all sit together. So after one game, Mark went to the club ticket office and asked about the availability of seat F12. However, he was told that the seat had been sold.

Even so, for week after week the seat remained empty until finally, on Boxing Day, it was taken for the first time that season. Mark and Jim were amazed and asked the new occupant: 'Where have you been all season?'

'Don't ask!' he said. 'My wife bought the season ticket back in the summer and kept it for a surprise Christmas present!'

'The one thing women don't want to find in their stockings on Christmas morning is their husband.'
JOAN RIVERS

A man asked his wife what she wanted for Christmas. 'Well,' she said optimistically, eyeing his brand new car parked on the drive, 'a little something to run around in would be nice.'

So he bought her a tracksuit.

'What would you like for Christmas, darling?' asked the husband. 'How about a new wardrobe full of designer label clothes?'

'No, I don't think so,' said the wife.

'How about a five-star, winter break in Bali?'

'No, I don't think so. You see, what I really want is a divorce.'

'A divorce?' gasped the husband. 'Sorry, darling, I wasn't planning to spend that much!'

I COULDN'T EAT ANOTHER THING

While the rest of the family were chatting in the lounge, the wife was busy in the kitchen preparing the Christmas dinner. As she lifted the turkey out of the oven to baste it, her husband suddenly appeared at her side.

'Careful!' he said. 'Not too much juice! You don't want to drench it! And don't forget the roast potatoes! Turn them! Turn them now! Now! Right now! Oh my God! They're going to stick! Slow things down a bit! Careful! Careful! I said be careful! You never listen to me when you're cooking! Never! Watch what you're doing! Quick! Your mind is wandering! Pay attention!'

His wife stared at him in disbelief. 'What the hell is wrong with you? Do you think I don't know how to cook Christmas dinner after all these years?'

The husband replied calmly: 'I just wanted you to know what it feels like when I'm driving.'

Instead of having Christmas dinner at home, a couple decided to book a table at their favourite Indian restaurant. Studying the menu, the husband asked the waiter: 'What's the Chicken Tarka?'

The waiter replied: 'It's like Chicken Tikka, but a little 'otter.'

Realizing that he would otherwise be alone at Christmas, a wife insisted on inviting her elderly uncle over to the family home to spend Christmas Day with them. Unfortunately, the uncle's digestive system could no longer cope with rich food the way it used to, with the result that he tended to break wind on a regular basis.

When everyone, including the couple's three children, sat down to Christmas dinner, the uncle attacked the Brussels sprouts with great enthusiasm. All too predictably, shortly afterwards a foul stench wafted into the air.

Sensing his embarrassment, the wife turned pointedly to the family dog, who was sitting next to the table, and said: 'Spike, move away, please.' The uncle was grateful to her for apportioning the blame elsewhere.

A minute or so later, the uncle released another ripper. Once again the considerate wife turned to the dog and said: 'Spike, move away, please.'

A couple of minutes later, the sprouts again took their toll. As the uncle squirmed, the wife bailed him out for a third time in front of the children, saying firmly: 'Spike, move away, please . . . now!'

No sooner had she finished speaking than the uncle struck again with his most pungent gas to date. This time the husband turned to the dog and said: 'For goodness' sake, Spike, hurry up and move before he craps all over you!'

Kevin hated his job as a waiter in a rundown restaurant, especially because it meant he had to work over Christmas. Towards the end of a long, busy Christmas Eve he had to serve a particularly awkward customer who had complained about everything – the position of his table, the cleanliness of the cutlery and the flavour of his soup. When it came to the main course, the customer ordered a steak and Kevin, by now way past caring, brought it to him with his thumb pressing down on the meat.

The customer was horrified. 'What are you doing putting your hand on my steak?'

'Well,' said Kevin, 'you wouldn't want it falling on the floor again.'

Alf and George were sitting in the pub and the conversation turned to Christmas dinner. Alf asked: 'Do you have roast turkey with all the trimmings?'

'Yes, every year,' replied George. 'My wife's a terrific cook.'

'You're lucky,' said Alf. 'Mine uses the smoke alarm as a cooking timer.'

YOU KNOW YOU'RE A BAD COOK WHEN ...

* Your homemade bread can be used as a doorstop.
* Your cat has only three lives left.
* Your kids' favourite drink is Alka-Seltzer.
* The local fire service cancels all leave when they know you're cooking.
* Your two best recipes are meatloaf and apple pie, but your guests can't tell which is which.
* It takes an industrial chisel to remove your homemade lasagne from the dish.
* Your gravy doesn't move.
* You get even with people who have annoyed you by inviting them over for dinner.
* Friends feel sorry for your taste buds.
* The three regular items on your dinner table are salt, pepper and stomach pump.
* Your pie filling bubbles over and eats the enamel off the bottom of the oven.
* Pest control companies keep calling you asking for your recipes.
* Your microwave displays 'Help!'
* Your dog goes to the neighbours' house to eat.

A wife said to her husband: 'I've baked two types of mince pies for Christmas. Would you like to take your pick?'

He said: 'No, I'll just use the hammer as usual.'

'I'm not saying my wife is a terrible cook, but our garbage disposal has developed an ulcer.'
HENNY YOUNGMAN

A seven-year-old boy was asked to say thanks for Christmas dinner. The family members bowed their heads in anticipation. He began his prayer, thanking God for his Mummy, Daddy, brother, sister, Grandma and all his aunts and uncles.

Then he began to thank God for the food. He gave thanks for the turkey, the stuffing, the roast potatoes, even the cranberry sauce, before pausing for what seemed like an age.

After a long silence, he finally looked up at his mother and said: 'If I thank God for the Brussels sprouts, won't he know I'm lying?'

A man was married to the worst cook in the world. One Christmas Eve he came home from work to find her in floods of tears.

'It's a disaster,' she wailed. 'The cat has eaten your dinner!'

'Don't worry,' he said. 'I'll buy you a new cat.'

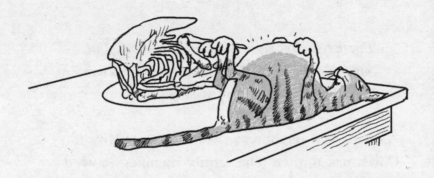

Before his in-laws arrived for Christmas dinner, a man asked his young son to set the table. But as everyone sat down to eat, the wife noticed that there was no cutlery at her father's place setting.

'Tommy, why didn't you give Grandpa a knife and fork?' she asked.

'I didn't think I needed to,' said the boy. 'I heard Dad say Grandpa always eats like a horse.'

A man answered the phone on Christmas morning. 'Yes, Mother,' he sighed. 'It's been a tough morning. Jane is in one of her difficult moods, panicking about how long it's going to take to cook the turkey . . . Yes, I know I ought to be firmer with her, but it's not easy. You know what she's like . . . Yes, I remember you warned me . . . Yes, I remember you told me she would make my life a misery . . . Yes, I remember you pleaded with me not to marry her. You were right . . . You want to speak to her? OK.'

He put the phone down and called to his wife in the kitchen: 'Jane, your mother wants to talk to you!'

Two friends were saying how much they looked forward to Christmas dinner. 'On a cold winter's day,' said one, 'there's nothing better than tucking into roast turkey with all the trimmings.'

'I agree,' said the other. 'And last year it was so cold my wife served pigs in electric blankets!'

At a remote mountain monastery, the monks operated a strict vow of silence, which was only allowed to be broken on Christmas Day, and even then only by one monk with just one sentence.

One Christmas, Brother Michael was permitted to speak and he said: 'I very much like the mashed potatoes we have with the turkey.' He then sat down and silence ensued for the next 365 days.

The following Christmas, it was Brother Timothy's turn to speak. He said: 'Personally, I thought the mashed potatoes were rather lumpy.' He then sat down and silence ensued for the next 365 days.

The next Christmas, Brother Matthew rose to his feet and said: 'I am fed up with this constant bickering.'

How can you tell when a turkey is done?

~

It flushes the toilet.

A young man was invited to spend Christmas Day at the luxury mansion owned by his girlfriend's parents. He had been raised in a modest, two-bedroom house so he felt somewhat intimidated by his first visit to this vast country estate staffed by maids and butlers.

Desperate not to commit a faux-pas, he made a point of only speaking when spoken to; even so, in the general chit-chat before lunch he felt he had acquitted himself rather well. Everyone had laughed at his jokes and all-in-all he was quietly pleased with himself.

Christmas lunch was an eight-course banquet, with all the guests seated around a huge antique wooden table. Again he did not put a foot wrong.

He avoided slurping his soup and used the correct cutlery for each course. However, the combination of rich food and champagne meant that about two-thirds of the way through the meal he felt an increasing urge to break wind. Not wishing to risk it at the dinner table, he asked to be excused to go to the bathroom and asked his girlfriend for directions.

These were by no means straightforward and required a lengthy walk involving a number of turns. After a few minutes, he realized he was hopelessly lost in the labyrinth of corridors and now urgently needed to release the build-up of internal gas. Spotting a window in the hallway, he decided to take a chance. He quickly pushed it open, shoved his butt through and released the volcanic build-up of gas. Relief was instant. He then closed the window and managed to retrace his steps to the dining room.

He sat down with a huge burden lifted from his shoulders, but noticed that everyone was strangely quiet. Trying to lift the mood, he whispered to his girlfriend: 'This is all going rather well, isn't it?'

'It was,' she said sternly, 'until you farted through the serving hatch!'

Ten members of the same family were seated around the table for Christmas lunch. After finishing the roast turkey they were finally ready for the dessert of Christmas pudding. The youngest son was keen to help his mother and proudly carried in the first slice, handing it to his father who passed it down the line to one of the guests.

A minute or so later, the boy came in with a second slice of Christmas pudding and handed it to his father who, in turn, passed it on to another guest. Seeing this, the boy said: 'It's no use, Dad. The pieces are all the same size!'

What's the difference between boogers
and Brussels sprouts?

Kids will eat boogers.

A couple who had been married for forty-nine years sat down to Christmas dinner with their eleven children. As the eldest raised a toast to the parents, he asked them the secret of how they had managed to stay together for so long.

'That's easy,' said the husband. 'Years ago we made a promise to each other: the first one to pack up and leave had to take all the kids.'

Two friends, Ted and Eric, went to the pub for Christmas lunch, which was taking the form of an outdoor festive barbecue. As soon as the chef put two steaks on the grill, Ted greedily picked the bigger one for himself.

Eric wasn't happy about it. 'When are you going to learn some common courtesy?' he said.

Showing no remorse, Ted answered: 'If you'd had the chance to pick first, which steak would you have chosen?'

'The smaller one, of course,' said Eric.

'Well then, what are you whining about?' said Ted. 'You've got the smaller one!'

The whole family was seated around the table for Christmas dinner when the youngest boy suddenly turned to his father and said: 'Dad, are maggots good to eat?'

'Don't be so disgusting,' said his father. 'I've told you before not to talk about things like that at the dinner table!'

A few minutes later when he had finished eating, the father, feeling guilty that he may have been a little harsh on his son in front of everyone, said: 'Now, son, what was it you wanted to know?'

'Oh, nothing,' said the boy. 'There was a maggot on your broccoli but now it's gone.'

'We were so poor, we couldn't afford a turkey.
So we gave the budgie chest expanders.'
LES DAWSON

On Christmas night, a woman woke her husband to say: 'I think there's a burglar downstairs and I can hear him eating the Christmas cake that mother made us.'

'Who do you want me to phone?' asked the husband. 'The police or an ambulance?'

At the family Christmas lunch, the son suddenly stood up to make an announcement. 'I've something to tell you all,' he began excitedly. 'Angie and I are getting married.'

His father's face fell. He took his son to one side and said: 'I'm sorry, son, you can't marry Angie. When I was first married to your mother, I'm afraid I fooled around a lot. You see, Angie is your half-sister.'

The son was devastated and it took him months to start dating again. But the following Christmas he had more good news to announce over lunch. 'Lauren and I are getting married.'

His father's face dropped. Once again he took his son to one side and explained: 'I'm sorry, son, you can't marry Lauren. She's your half-sister, too.'

The son ran to his room in tears. Later his mother came up to comfort him.

'Dad's done a lot of bad things,' sobbed the son. 'He keeps saying I can't marry the girl I love.'

'Oh, don't pay any attention to him,' she said. 'He's not your real father.'

A new bride called her mother in floods of tears on Christmas Eve. She sobbed: 'James just doesn't appreciate what I do for him.'

'I'm sure that's not true,' said her mother trying to comfort her. 'It was probably all just a misunderstanding.'

'No, Mother, it wasn't. You see, I bought a frozen turkey roll for Christmas dinner tomorrow and he yelled and screamed at me about the price.'

'Well, what a cheapskate!' said the mother. 'Those turkey rolls are only a few dollars.'

'No, Mother, it wasn't the price of the turkey. It was the airplane ticket.'

'Airplane ticket? Why did you need an airplane ticket?'

'Well, Mother, when I read the packaging, it said "prepare from a frozen state". So I flew to Alaska.'

A couple booked a table for two at a smart restaurant for Christmas lunch. When their food arrived, the husband said: 'Great. Let's eat. I'm starving!'
His wife reminded him: 'But you always say your prayers at home before dinner.'
The husband replied: 'That's at home. Here the chef knows how to cook.'

Grandpa was showing his young grandson around the farm on Christmas morning. When they came to the corral, Grandpa explained to the boy: 'That's a bull and a cow, and he's serving her.'

Shortly afterwards, they saw two horses. Grandpa said: 'That's a stallion and a mare, and he's serving her, too.'

At Christmas dinner, after everyone was settled in their seats and grace was said, Grandma turned to Grandpa and said: 'Will you please serve the turkey?'

The grandson jumped to his feet and yelled: 'If he does, I'm eating a burger!'

The seven-year-old son was asked to pray before the family's Christmas dinner. He said: 'Dear God, please, please send clothes for all those poor ladies on Dad's computer. Amen.'

For Boxing Day evening, a wife decided to prepare a simple buffet for her guests. Not being a virtuoso in the kitchen, this meant opening a couple of packets of crisps and attempting to make a few sandwiches. But her husband took one bite out of a sandwich and immediately spat it out.

'Ugh!' he spluttered. 'What's in that sandwich?'

'Why?' she said.

'Because it's disgusting. What's in it?'

'Crab paste.'

'Well, I've never tasted anything that bad in my life. Where did you buy it?'

'The pharmacy.'

'I love the holiday season.
See ya in spring, toes.'
HOMER SIMPSON,
THE SIMPSONS

Rather than buy ready-made sausage rolls for Christmas, a wife decided to save money by baking her own. She laboured over the recipe for hours and although most came out of the oven with an odd shape, she was quietly proud of her achievement. Asking her husband to taste one, she waited eagerly for his verdict. When none was forthcoming, she said: 'If I baked these commercially, what do you think I could get for them?'

'About twelve years,' he replied stonily.

WHO THINKS UP THIS STUFF?

If there is one thing that everyone agrees on at Christmas it is how lame Christmas cracker jokes are. Yet perversely, rather like Brussels sprouts, some of us just can't get enough of them. Indeed some Christmases are so grim that the highlight of the whole period can be pulling a cracker to find that it contains the fortune-telling fish and a riddle about what a frog does if his car breaks down. (Spoiler alert, he gets it toad away). Here are some more cracker jokes to make you cringe:

*Why are real Christmas trees like
clumsy knitters?*

They both drop their needles.

Who hides in a bakery at Christmas?

A mince spy.

~

*What's the difference between Santa
and a warm dog?*

**Santa wears a whole suit, a warm
dog just pants.**

Why are photographers so depressed?

**Because they always focus on the
negatives.**

*What Christmas carol do they sing
in the desert?*

'O Camel Ye Faithful'.

~

*How do you stop your mouth from freezing
at Christmas?*

Grit your teeth.

What do reindeer want for Christmas?

A Pony Sleigh Station.

~

Why don't pawns give to charity?

Because they're shellfish.

How do snowmen get around?

They ride an icicle.

*What happened to the man who fell into
an upholstery machine?*

He is fully recovered.

~

*What did Adam say the day before
Christmas?*

'It's Christmas, Eve.'

~

*What happened when the glassblower
inhaled?*

He got a pane in the stomach.

What do you call a snowman in summer?

A puddle.

~

How do we know Santa is good at karate?

Because he has a black belt.

What do you call an unemployed jester?

Nobody's fool.

~

*What happened when Santa got stuck
in the chimney?*

He felt Claustrophobic.

How do you make an apple crumble?

Torture it for ten minutes.

*Why did nobody bid for Donner and
Blitzen on eBay?*

They were two deer.

~

Why did the two pythons get married?

Because they had a crush on each other.

~

*What happened to the man who stole
an advent calendar?*

He got twenty-five days.

*Why is it becoming so difficult to
buy advent calendars?*

Their days are numbered.

*What falls at the North Pole but
never gets hurt?*

Snow.

~

*What happened to the man who was sacked
from operating the dodgems?*

He sued for funfair dismissal.

~

What is Rudolph's favourite day of the year?

Red Nose Day

Why is the letter T like an island?

Because it's in the middle of water.

*What did Cinderella say when her
photos didn't arrive?*

'Some day my prints will come.'

~

What do you get if you lie under a cow?

A pat on the head.

~

Why did Santa put a clock in his sleigh?

He wanted to see time fly.

*What do you get when you cross a fish
and an elephant?*

Swimming trunks.

*What did one snowman say to the
other snowman?*

'Can you smell carrots?'

~

*How did the three wise men figure out Jesus
was exactly 6lbs 9oz when he was born?*

They had a weigh in a manger.

~

Why did the man stamp on his watch?

Because he had time to kill.

Which side of a turkey has the most feathers?

The outside.

~

How much does it cost Santa to park his sleigh and reindeer?

Nothing. It's on the house.

~

What do you call a boomerang that doesn't come back?

A stick.

What's the difference between a knight and Santa Claus?

One slays a dragon, the other drags a sleigh.

How does Darth Vader enjoy his Christmas turkey?

On the dark side.

~

What is so fragile that even saying its name can break it?

Silence.

~

What do you get if you eat Christmas decorations?

Tinselitis.

203

*What did Geronimo cry as he jumped
out of the airplane?*

'Me!!!!!!!'

~

*How did Scrooge score the winning goal in the
football match?*

The ghost of Christmas passed.

~

What did the hat say to the scarf?

'You hang around while I go on ahead.'

~

*What did the bald man say when he got a
comb for Christmas?*

'Thanks, I'll never part with it.'

*Why couldn't the skeleton go to
the Christmas party?*

Because he had no body to go with.

~

*Which Disney film features lots of swearing
and cursing?*

101 Damnations.

~

*What starts with E, ends with E but
usually has only one letter?*

An envelope.

~

*Why did Cinderella never make it
as a footballer?*

**She kept running away
from the ball.**

What was the other reason why Cinderella wasn't any good at football?

Her coach was a pumpkin.

Why did the man put his money in the freezer?

Because he wanted cold, hard cash.

~

How did the bauble get addicted to Christmas?

He was hooked on trees his whole life.

~

What's red and white, red and white, red and white?

Santa rolling off your roof.

Why did the turkey get picked to be in a band?

He was the only one with drumsticks.

~

Why did the baby strawberry cry?

Because his mother was in a jam.

*Why does Santa enjoy working
in the garden?*

**Because he likes to
hoe, hoe, hoe.**

*Why don't human cannonballs keep their
jobs for very long?*

**Because as soon as they start
they get fired.**

*Why was Santa's little helper feeling
depressed?*

Because he had low elf esteem.

~

What do you call Santa's helpers?

Subordinate Clauses.

~

Why did the little girl put lipstick on her head?

She wanted to make up her mind.

What did Mrs Claus say to Santa when she looked up in the sky?

'Looks like rain, dear.'

~

Who earns a living by driving his customers away?

A taxi driver.

How does Santa keep track of all the fireplaces he has visited?

He keeps a logbook.

~

What did the big chimney say to the small chimney?

'You're too young to smoke.'

*How did Darth Vader know what
Luke Skywalker was getting for Christmas?*

He felt his presents.

What has four wheels and flies?

A garbage truck.

~

*What do you get from sitting on
snow too long?*

Polaroids.

~

*How many chimneys does Santa Claus
go down?*

Stacks.

*What is it that even the most careful
person overlooks?*

His nose.

What's round and bad-tempered?

A vicious circle.

~

Why does Dick Whittington have a beard?

**Because nine out of ten owners know
their cats prefer whiskers.**

~

What's full of holes but still holds water?

A sponge.

Who is Santa's favourite singer?

Elfis Presley.

~

*Why does Scrooge love Rudolph the
red-nosed reindeer?*

**Because every buck is
precious to him.**

What did the postcard say to the stamp?

'Stick with me and we'll go places.'

What happened to the turkey that got in a fight?

He had the stuffing knocked out of him.

What do you call a blind reindeer?

No-eye deer.

~

What do you get if you cross a pig and a telephone?

A lot of crackling on the line.

Why was the snowman sad?

Because he had a meltdown.

~

What did one plate say to the other plate?

'Lunch is on me.'

*Why was the snowman embarrassed when he
was spotted rummaging through a
bag of carrots?*

Because he was caught picking his nose.

~

What do you call a fly without wings?

A walk.

*Why has Santa been banned from
sooty chimneys?*

Because of his carbon footprints.

~

Why are pirates called pirates?

Because they arrrrrr.

*How many letters are there in the
alphabet at Christmas?*

Twenty-five; there's no-el.

~

*What do they sing at a snowman's
birthday party?*

'Freeze a jolly good fellow'.

Why does your nose get tired in winter?

It runs all day.

Why did the tightrope walker go to the ATM?

To check his balance.

~

Why do mummies love Christmas?

Because of all the wrapping.

What did the shy pebble say?

'I wish I was a little boulder.'

~

Why are horse-drawn carriages so unpopular?

**Because horses are rubbish
at drawing.**

WHO THINKS UP THIS STUFF?

What kind of motorbike does Santa ride?

A Holly Davidson.

What is the best Christmas present?

A broken drum; you can't beat it.

~

Who makes suits and eats spinach?

Popeye the Tailorman.

What do you call a dancing turkey?

Poultry in motion.

~

What do you call the soft tissue between a shark's teeth?

The slow swimmer.

What does Santa do when his elves misbehave?

He gives them the sack.

~

Why do birds fly south in the winter?

Because it's too far to walk.

What did the mother turkey say to her disobedient children?

'If your father could see you now, he'd turn in his gravy!'

~

What's an ig?

A snow house without a loo.

~

What goes Oh, Oh, Oh?

Santa walking backwards.

What goes Ho, Ho, Ho, Thump?

Santa laughing his head off.

What does Miley Cyrus have for her Christmas dinner?

Twerky.

What did the traffic light say to the car?

'Don't look, I'm changing.'

~

What do you call a snowman with a six pack?

An abdominal snowman.

Why did the man tiptoe past the medicine cabinet?

He didn't want to wake the sleeping pills.

What do you get when you cross a snowman with a vampire?

Frostbite.

~

Why did the scarecrow get a big Christmas bonus?

Because he was outstanding in his field.

~

What happened when the snowlady fell out with the snowman?

She gave him the cold shoulder.

Why did the pony have to gargle?

Because it was a little horse.

What do you give a dog for Christmas?

A mobile bone.

~

What does a snowman take when he gets sick?

A chill pill.

What are never built to scale?

Prison walls.

~

*What's worse than Rudolph with a
runny nose?*

Frosty the snowman with a hot flush.

When is a boat just like snow?

When it's adrift.

*What did the big candle say to the
little candle?*

'I'm going out for dinner tonight.'

~

What do snowmen wear on their heads?

Ice caps.

Why don't dogs make good dancers?

Because they have two left feet.

~

What goes Ho Ho Whoosh, Ho Ho Whoosh?

Santa going through a revolving door.

Why do ghosts make bad liars?

Because you can see right through them.

How does Good King Wenceslas like his pizzas?

Deep pan, crisp and even.

~

How can you get four suits for £1?

Buy a pack of cards.

What's the most popular Christmas wine?

'I don't like sprouts!'

~

What do you get if you cross Christmas with a duck?

A Christmas quacker.

THE CHRISTMAS SPIRIT

A man came home drunk after enjoying a few Christmas drinks with friends. As he stumbled through the front door, desperate not to wake his wife, he walked into the corner of a shelf in the hallway, the impact leaving blood trickling down his face. He went straight to the bathroom to try and heal the wound before sliding into bed.

The next morning his wife said: 'You came home drunk last night, didn't you?'

'No,' he replied, mustering all the sincerity at his disposal.

'Then perhaps,' she continued, 'you can explain to me why there are plasters all over the bathroom mirror?'

A wife was lying in bed on the morning after Boxing Day when she heard a commotion in the kitchen. She went downstairs to find her husband slumped at the table stinking of beer and with lipstick on his collar.

'I hope you've got a good reason for turning up here at seven o'clock in the morning!' she boomed.

'I have,' he said. 'Breakfast.'

'Next to a circus there ain't nothing that packs up and tears out of town any quicker than the Christmas spirit.'
KIN HUBBARD

Alex turned to his partner Jane and said: 'Is the Exorcist coming this Christmas?'

'Who's the Exorcist?' asked Jane, baffled.

'Bill – your father.'

'Why do you call him the Exorcist?

'Because every time he comes to visit he makes the spirits disappear.'

Despite drinking for most of Christmas Eve, a man foolishly decided to drive home from the pub. His erratic driving soon attracted the attention of a police patrol car and an officer pulled him over and asked him to take a breathalyser test.

'I can't,' said the man. 'You see I have very bad asthma and breathing into that device could trigger an attack.'

'OK,' said the officer, 'then you'll have to take a blood test.'

'I can't do that either,' said the man. 'I'm a haemophiliac. If a wound is opened, I won't stop bleeding and could bleed to death.'

'Very well,' said the officer, becoming increasingly frustrated, 'I'll take a urine sample.'

'Sorry, can't do that,' said the man. 'I also have diabetes. Giving a urine sample could push my sugar count dangerously low.'

'Right,' said the officer firmly. 'Then the only thing for it is for you to get out of the car and walk in a straight line for me, say from here to that hedge.'

'No, I can't do that,' said the man.

'Why not?' the officer asked, more exasperated than ever.

'Because I'm drunk.'

Late on Christmas Eve, a drunk was on his knees beneath a street light, apparently searching for something. Since it was Christmas, a passer-by offered to help. 'What is it that you have lost?' he asked.

'My watch,' replied the drunk. 'It fell off when I tripped over the kerb.'

So the passer-by joined in the search, but after twenty minutes there was still no sign of the watch.

'Where exactly did you trip?' asked the passer-by.

'About half a block away,' replied the drunk.

'Then why are you looking for your watch here if you lost it half a block further up the street?'

The drunk said: 'Because the light's a lot better here.'

A police officer spotted a drunk wandering the streets at four o'clock on Christmas morning. 'Can you explain why you're out at this hour?' asked the officer.

The drunk replied: 'If I could, I'd be home by now!'

A teenage girl got very drunk on Christmas Eve and had to stay overnight at a friend's house. It wasn't until the following morning that she was sober enough to call her parents to let them know she was safe and well.

'Dad, it's Ellie,' she said. 'Just to let you know I'm fine. I knew you'd be worried, but I didn't get a chance to call you last night. It was past midnight when we left the bar and I had to stay at Louise's house. And it was so late I didn't want to disturb you because I knew you'd both be asleep. Please don't be mad at me.'

By now, the man on the other end of the phone realized that the caller had got the wrong number. 'I'm sorry,' he said, 'I don't have a daughter named Ellie.'

'Gee, Dad, I didn't think you'd be this mad!'

On Christmas Eve night, a man walked into a bar and ordered a martini. The bartender brought him his drink, whereupon the man fished out the olive and put it in a jar. After downing the drink, he ordered another and did the same thing. An hour later, he was considerably the worse for wear and had a pile of olives in the jar.

'Excuse me,' said the bartender, eyeing the jar, 'but why do you keep doing that?'

'Well, you see,' said the man, nearly falling off his stool, 'my wife sent me out for a jar of olives and all the shops are closed.'

After losing touch when they were young, Ken and Peter met up for a Christmas drink – their first meeting in over twenty years. 'So how's life been treating you?' asked Peter.

'One disaster after another, I'm afraid,' replied Ken. 'My wife was killed in a freak skiing accident, then two years later my eldest boy was fatally struck by lightning. Then my house burned to the ground in a mystery fire, and my youngest boy died after being hit in the head by a stray golf ball. My dog was run over, my sister drowned at sea and three months ago my doctor told me I had an incurable disease. And to cap it all, my business has just gone bust.'

'Gee! That all sounds terrible,' said Peter. 'What business are you in?'

Ken replied: 'I sell lucky charms.'

'Christmas at my house is always at least six or seven times more pleasant than anywhere else. We start drinking early. And while everyone else is seeing only one Santa Claus, we'll be seeing six or seven.'
W.C. FIELDS

Early on Christmas morning, three drunks were riding home on one motorcycle. As they passed a stationary police patrol car, the officer yelled at them: 'Stop immediately!'

But instead they continued on their merry way and, as they weaved erratically along the street, the guy at the back turned around and shouted to the officer: 'Sorry, mate. There's not room for you. We're already carrying one too many!'

When a man came home drunk at two o'clock on Christmas morning, his wife was waiting to confront him. 'I told you two beers and home by ten o'clock,' she raged.

'Sorry,' he said. 'I must have got the numbers mixed up.'

A couple went out for a celebratory drink on Christmas night.

'What would you like?' he asked her.

'Champagne, I guess.'

'Guess again,' he said.

A married couple were driving home from a Christmas night out when they were stopped by the police. 'Sir,' said the officer, 'did you know you were speeding?'

'No,' said the husband, 'I had no idea. I'm always very careful about keeping within the limit. It must have been a momentary lapse.'

'What are you talking about?' said his wife. 'You're always speeding. You see it as a challenge.'

The officer then walked to the back of the vehicle and said: 'Sir, did you know your brake light is broken?'

'No,' said the husband. 'I had no idea that it was broken. I always check for that sort of thing, so it must have happened very recently.'

'Nonsense,' interrupted the wife. 'It's been broken for weeks. I kept telling you to get it fixed but you're too mean to part with any money for the repairs.'

The husband had heard enough and rounded on his wife: 'Shut up, you stupid woman. Why can't you keep your mouth shut for once?'

The officer was appalled by his tone and said to the wife: 'Does he always talk to you like that?'

'No,' she said, 'only when he's drunk.'

Two men were sitting at a bar on Christmas Eve. One started to insult the other, screaming: 'I slept with your mother!'

The bar fell silent as everyone waited to see how the other man would react. Then the first man repeated the taunt: 'I slept with your mother!'

The second man rose to his feet, grabbed the first man by the collar and said: 'Let's go home, Dad. You've had too much to drink!'

Two men had been drinking in the pub non-stop for the whole of Christmas Eve. Late in the evening, one turned to the other and said: 'Have you any idea what time it is?'

'No,' said the other, 'but it can't be ten o'clock.'

'How do you know?'

'Well, because my wife said I was to be home by ten o'clock and I'm not.'

A wife was in bed with her lover on Christmas Eve when she heard her husband's key in the door. He was returning from the pub where he had been for the past twelve hours.

'Don't panic,' the wife told her lover. 'Stay where you are. He's so drunk he won't even notice you're in bed with me.'

Sure enough, the husband lurched into the bedroom and fell into bed none the wiser. But then a couple of minutes later, in a drunken haze, he counted six feet sticking out at the end of the bed. Turning to his wife, he said: 'What's going on? There are six feet in this bed. There should only be four.'

'What are you talking about?' said the wife. 'You're so drunk you can't count or see properly. Get out of bed, stand by the window and try again. The light is better over there.'

So the husband climbed out of bed and counted again. 'One, two, three, four. Oh, OK, you were right ...'

A traffic cop stopped a drunk driver in the early hours of Christmas morning. 'Excuse me, sir,' said the officer, peering into the driver's side window, 'have you been drinking?'

'Sure I have,' replied the driver. 'I had four pints of Guinness with my pals at lunchtime and then I spent the afternoon in the Irish Bar, drinking Guinness with whisky chasers. During Happy Hour I downed five double brandies and then I had a couple of drinks with old friends, just to be sociable. And then I drove one of my friends home and had a few cans of beer at his house because it would have been rude to refuse at this time of year."

'I see,' said the officer. 'I'm afraid I'm going to have to ask you to step out of the car and take a breathalyser test.'

'What's the matter?' said the drunk. 'Don't you believe me?'

'That's the true spirit of Christmas; people being helped by people other than me.'
JERRY SEINFELD

Every night for a week on the run-up to Christmas, a husband went out and got drunk before coming home at midnight to a frosty reception from his wife. She told a friend about how awkward the atmosphere had become at home as a result of his constant drinking, prompting the friend to suggest a different approach. The friend advised that instead of haranguing him when he got in, she should shower him with kindness.

So that night when he staggered in late as usual, he was greeted with a friendly kiss. She sat him in his favourite chair, brought him his slippers and made him a nice cup of tea. He could hardly believe it. Where were the insults and accusations? It was all so different. After a while she said: 'It's getting late now, darling. I think we'd best go upstairs to bed.'

'We might as well,' he said, slurring his words. 'I'll be in trouble when I get home anyway.'

When the last of their Christmas guests had gone, a couple celebrated by going out to a restaurant for dinner. As the wife studied the wine menu, she said: 'This one is described as full-bodied and imposing with a nutty base, a sharp bite and a bitter aftertaste.' The husband said: 'Are you describing the wine or your mother?'

Chris came home very drunk after hitting a few bars on Christmas Eve. When he finally made it into bed, he prodded his sleeping wife and said: 'Jen, Jen, wake up! Guess what just happened?'

'No idea,' said his wife groggily.

'Well,' he continued, 'I went to the toilet and the light switched on all by itself. And then when I left, the light switched off again without me having to do a thing. I think I'm developing super powers!'

'No, Chris, you idiot!' she sighed. 'You just peed into the fridge again!'

Two drunks were drowning their sorrows at home at Christmas. After a while, as the conversation grew increasingly maudlin, one reached into his drinks cabinet and said: 'If I die before you, will you pour this bottle of whisky on my grave?'

The other stared at the bottle longingly and replied: 'Sure I will. But would you mind if I passed it through my kidneys first?'

One Christmas Eve, a man was on his way home from work when he was stopped by a beggar with tattered clothes, long, unkempt hair and a straggly beard that nearly stretched down to his navel.

'Could you lend me £5 as it's Christmas?' he pleaded.

'Will you spend it on booze?' asked the man.

'Definitely not,' said the beggar.

'Will you gamble it away?' asked the man.

'No, sir, I definitely won't,' replied the beggar.

'In that case I'd like you to come home with me so my wife can see what happens to a man who doesn't drink or gamble.'

Three grumpy old men were sitting in a bar at Christmas.

The first said: 'I hate everything about being old. One of the worst things is I can't even enjoy a good pee anymore.'

The second agreed: 'I know what you mean. I hate being old, too. Remember when you were young and were able to take a big healthy dump every day? What I wouldn't give to be able to do that now!'

The third man said: 'Well, fellas, I have to say that every morning, regular as clockwork, I take a good pee at six o'clock. And every morning at seven o'clock I take a big, lovely, healthy dump.' Then he let out a long sigh before adding: 'I just wish I could wake up before eight o'clock.'

YOU KNOW YOU'VE HAD TOO MUCH TO DRINK AT CHRISTMAS WHEN ...

* Your doctor finds traces of blood in your alcohol stream.
* You can focus better with one eye closed.
* You ask carol singers for an encore.
* You lose arguments with inanimate objects.
* You start playing footsie at the dinner table with your maiden aunt.
* The back of your head keeps getting hit by the toilet seat.
* Mosquitoes get a buzz after biting you.
* Brussels sprouts start to taste good.
* Your favourite bar's profits drop by fifty per cent if you're staying with relatives over Christmas.
* You get home, put food in the microwave, and then enter your PIN number.
* Christmas Day and Boxing Day merge into one.
* You have to hold on to the floor to keep from sliding off.
* Everyone you look at appears to have a twin.
* You laugh at your Christmas cracker joke.

A man walked into a bar on Christmas Eve and said to the bartender: 'It's Christmas. So a beer for me, a beer for you and a beer for everyone else!'

The bartender served the drinks but after downing his beer, the man headed for the door.

'Hey, you haven't paid for all those drinks!' cried the bartender.

'I haven't got any money,' explained the man.

The bartender was furious and gave him a good kicking before throwing him out on the street.

The next evening the man returned to the same bar. 'It's Christmas!' he shouted to the bartender. 'So a beer for me, a beer for you and a beer for everyone else!'

The bartender didn't think the man would be stupid enough to pull the same stunt twice, so he served the beers as requested. But again, after drinking his beer, the man prepared to leave.

'Not so fast!' screamed the bartender. 'You haven't paid for the drinks you ordered!'

'I don't have any money,' said the man.

Angrier than ever, the bartender gave him an even more severe kicking than before and threw him out on the street.

The following evening, the man returned to the bar once more. 'It's Christmas!' he yelled to the bartender. 'So a beer for me and a beer for everyone else!'

'What, no beer for me this time?' said the bartender.

'No,' answered the man. 'You get violent when you drink.'

'I was coming out of my off-licence with four crates of lager, two crates of wine, a bottle of brandy and a bottle of vodka, and I said to the guy: "Christmas is really about the children, isn't it?"'
BARRY CRYER

After getting horribly drunk on Christmas Eve, a man kept bumping into people while making his way to his seat, and there were dark mutterings among the congregation about the state he was in. His behaviour and appearance left a lot to be desired. In fact he was so hungover and tired that he nodded off partway through the service.

The preacher watched him with barely concealed disgust until, at the end of the sermon, he decided to make an example of the man.

Addressing the congregation, the preacher said: 'All those wishing to have a place in heaven, please stand.'

The whole church stood up, except for the sleeping man. At the preacher's command, they then sat down again.

Then the preacher announced loudly: 'All those who would like a place in hell, please STAND UP!'

Jolted awake but only catching the last part, the man rose groggily to his feet. Confused and embarrassed to see that the rest of the congregation were seated, he said: 'I don't know what we're voting on here, Reverend, but it seems like you and me are the only ones in favour!'

After drinking way too much on Christmas Day, a man started to feel seriously ill. Eventually, he said to his wife: 'I think you'd better call me an ambulance.'

Picking up his phone, she said: 'Quick. Give me your password.'

'Never mind,' he said, in a sudden state of panic. 'I'm feeling much better now.'

A couple were relaxing together on Christmas evening sipping wine and watching TV.

Suddenly the wife whispered: 'I love you.'

The husband turned to her and said: 'Is that you or the wine talking?'

She said: 'It's me talking to the wine.'

A woman strongly disapproved of the fact that her husband spent almost every night at the pub. She herself hardly drank alcohol and so rarely joined him but, one Christmas, in an attempt to be sociable, she agreed to go with him.

'What would you like to drink?' he inquired as they reached the bar.

'Oh, I don't know,' she said. 'Just get me whatever you're having.'

She then took a seat while he ordered two whiskies. When he brought the drinks to their table, he downed his whisky in a single gulp but she took one sip of hers and immediately spat it out.

'Oh my God! That's vile!' she exclaimed. 'How can you drink this stuff?!'

'Well, there you go,' grinned the husband. 'And all this time you thought I was out enjoying myself every night!'

WELL, THIS IS FUN

A man's miserable Christmas was exacerbated by the sounds of music and laughter coming from the house next door for the whole of the evening, and into the early hours. The next morning he grumpily accosted his neighbour and said: 'Did you hear me thumping on the wall last night?'

'No, I didn't,' said the neighbour, 'but don't worry about it. We were making a fair bit of noise ourselves.'

What does Donald Trump do after he pulls a cracker?

~

He pays her off.

Desperate to escape the house at last after being stuck indoors entertaining relatives for three days over Christmas, a couple decided to go into town for a few drinks. They put on their best clothes, called a cab, and put the cat out. The taxi arrived but as the couple walked out the front door, the cat darted between their legs, back into the house and up the stairs. Knowing full well that the cat, if left alone, would wreck the house in their absence, the husband ran upstairs to chase the cat out again while the wife waited in the taxi.

Since she didn't want the cab driver to know that the house would be left unoccupied, she explained to him: 'My husband has just gone upstairs to say goodbye to my mother.'

A few minutes later, the husband reappeared and climbed into the taxi. 'Sorry I took so long,' he said. 'Stupid old thing was hiding under the bed, and I had to poke her with a coat hanger to get her to come out!'

'My Christmas decorations are inflatable. I'm forever blowing baubles.'
TIM VINE

A cannibal was invited to a teambuilding week in the mountains over the Christmas period. The invitation said he could also bring one friend, but when he arrived at the rendezvous point he had eight people with him.

'What's going on, Keith?' said the organizer. 'The invitation clearly stated that you could only bring one person.'

'Yeah, but it also said bring your own food, didn't it?'

Following a major row with his wife, Tim booked a room in a hotel on Christmas night, but was warned by the receptionist that the guest in the adjoining room was highly nervous and had difficulty getting to sleep. On reaching his room, Tim was so exhausted after a long and emotional day that he thoughtlessly threw his shoe down on the floor very hard. He immediately remembered the nervous guest in the next room, so he laid the other shoe down very gently without making a sound.

He then went to bed, but two hours later was woken by a knock at the door. He asked who it was and a voice replied: 'I'm the guest in the next room. For heaven's sake, throw that other shoe down, will you!'

A British couple went on an African safari at Christmas. Two of the guides set off ahead of the party of tourists to look for wildlife. One guide was carrying a rifle, the other a huge boulder. After a while the couple approached the two guides and asked them about their different approaches to the task.

'Why do you have a rifle on your back?' they asked the first guide.

'Because if a wild animal charges at me, I can fire the rifle into the air and scare it off.'

'That makes sense,' they agreed. 'And what about you?' they asked the second guide. 'Why do you carry that heavy boulder around with you?'

'Because,' he replied, 'if a wild animal charges at me, I can drop the boulder and run away much faster.'

While spending another lonely Christmas at home, a man decided to join a dating agency. But his luck didn't improve and, following a series of unsuccessful dates, he went back to the agency and pleaded with the proprietor: 'Have you got someone on your books who doesn't care what I look like, isn't concerned about my personal hygiene and has a lovely big pair of boobs?'

The proprietor checked the computer database and said: 'Actually, sir, we do have one. But it's you.'

Exiting church on Christmas morning, a man stopped at the door to speak to the vicar. 'Would it be right,' he asked, 'for a person to profit from the mistakes of another?'

'No, it would not be right,' said the vicar. 'Definitely not.'

'In that case,' said the man, 'I wonder if you would consider returning the £150 I paid you to marry me and my wife last June?'

On Christmas evening, a man and a woman were lying in bed together when she heard a noise coming from downstairs. 'Quick!' she said, half-asleep. 'It's my husband. You have to leave!'

Grabbing his clothes he leaped out of bed, scrambled through the window, jumped to the ground and clambered through a clump of bushes to reach the street. Then he suddenly stopped in his tracks as he realized something. Returning to the house, he said to the woman: 'Wait a minute! I AM your husband!'

She looked at him sternly and asked: 'So why did you run?'

Another Christmas offered the perfect opportunity for two friends to discuss the passing years and how middle age was starting to creep up on them.

One said: 'I've noticed that these days if I kneel down for something, it takes a few moments before I can stand up again. That's a definite sign of ageing.'

'Tell me about it,' said the other. 'I discovered my first grey pubic hair the other day.'

'Really?'

'Yeah, I got quite excited, but not as much as the other people in the elevator.'

A couple spent Christmas on their yacht off the coast of Australia. After they had travelled a few miles out to sea, the husband asked his wife: 'Do you want to go swimming?'

'I can't,' she said. 'I'm on my period.'

'Damn!' he moaned. 'You always take the fun out of shark fishing.'

A husband with six children decided one day that he would call his wife 'Mother of Six' all the time rather than address her by her real name. At first, she found it quite amusing but after a few months the joke began to wear thin and she grew tired of him saying things like, 'Mother of Six, what's for dinner?' or 'Mother of Six, fetch me a beer.'

Matters came to a head at a neighbour's Christmas party. Ready to leave, the husband called across the packed room: 'Mother of Six, it's time to go!'

Finally releasing her pent-up frustration, she shouted back: 'I'll be right with you, Father of Four!'

One Christmas, Jack ran into an old schoolmate.

'Al, how are you doing?' he asked.

'Yeah, great,' said Al. 'I'm a fireman.'

'Really? My fifteen-year-old son wants to be a fireman,' said Jack.

'Well, if you want some advice, install a pole in your house that will extend down to the basement so your kid can practise, because the hardest thing for a fireman is to jump off into space and catch that pole in the middle of the night.'

'Thanks for the tip, Al, I might do that.'

Seven years later, they met up again at Christmas.

'Did you install that pole in your house as I suggested?' asked Al.

'Yes, I did,' replied Jack.

'And did your son become a fireman?'

'No, he chose a different career. But I have two daughters who are dancers.'

On Christmas Day, a man was pouring himself a beer in the kitchen while his wife was watching TV. Suddenly he heard her shouting at the screen: 'No, don't do it . . . Don't enter that building . . . Turn around and walk away before it's too late . . . Oh, you stupid woman!'

'What are you watching?' he called out.

'Our wedding video,' she replied.

Two friends drove into town on Christmas Eve. As the car approached a red light, instead of stopping, the driver put his foot down on the gas and sped through.

'You just went through a red light,' said his passenger, shocked.

'Don't worry about it,' said the driver. 'My brother does it all the time.'

A minute or so later, they came to another red light and once again the driver hurtled through without stopping.

'What are you doing?' cried his passenger.

'That's another red light you missed! You're crazy!'

'Don't worry,' said the driver. 'My brother does it all the time.'

A couple of minutes later, they approached another red light and again the driver put his foot down and sped through without stopping.

'That's a third red light!' screamed the passenger. 'You're going to get us both killed!'

'You worry too much,' said the driver. 'My brother does it all the time.'

Shortly afterwards, they came to a green light but this time the driver slammed on his brakes.

'What the hell is up with you?!' said the passenger. 'You speed through three red lights without stopping and then you slam on the brakes when you come to a green light! What's going on?'

'I couldn't take any chances,' explained the driver. 'I had to stop. My brother might have been coming.'

Two old friends met up one Christmas after not seeing each other for over a decade.

'What are you doing these days?' asked the first.

'Phd,' replied the other.

'Wow! You're a doctor!'

'No, pizza home delivery.'

A man bought a theatre ticket for the Boxing Day production of a murder mystery play, but when taking his seat he found that his view was partly obscured by a pillar. So he summoned the usher and asked if he could be moved to another seat. 'There'll be a nice tip in it for you,' the man promised.

A couple of minutes later, the usher returned and discreetly led him to a more expensive seat with a much better view of the stage. The man then handed the usher a £1 coin. The usher looked at it disdainfully, leaned over and whispered in the man's ear: 'The butler did it.'

While the humans in the house were enjoying the festive period, two mice below the floorboards also met for a catch-up. 'Look,' said one, showing a photo on her mobile phone, 'I've got a new boyfriend. What do you think?'

'OMG!' cried the other mouse. 'That's a bat!'

'What?!' said the first mouse. 'The guy told me he was a pilot!'

John set up his friend Nick on a blind date with a girl on Boxing Day evening. Nick was worried about going on a date with someone he had never met before and asked John: 'What do I do if I find her really unattractive? I could be stuck with her for the whole evening.'

'Don't worry,' said John. 'In the unlikely event that you won't like what you see, there's a Bad

Date Rescue App that you can download to your smartphone. Schedule your phone to ring two minutes after you meet her and if you need to escape, just answer with: "Mom, what's the matter? Are you OK?" Then you make your excuses and leave. It's foolproof.'

Reassured, Nick went on the date as planned. He arrived at the girl's house and knocked on the door. As she came out, he was delighted to see that she was absolutely gorgeous, the girl of his dreams. But before he could express his approval, her phone rang and she answered with: 'Mom, what's the matter? Are you OK?'

With the house to themselves at last, a husband turned to his wife on the night after Boxing Day and said: 'Put your coat on, dear, I'm heading into town.'

'Oh, are you taking me out for a drink?' she asked excitedly.

'Don't be silly. I'm turning the central heating off.'

Why does it take longer to build a chav
snowman than a regular one?

~

Because you have to hollow out the head.

Three friends – Scott, Matt and Henry – booked into a hotel over Christmas, but after checking in at reception they discovered that the lift was out of order and that they would have to climb forty-eight flights of stairs to their room. Scott suggested that to make the long climb more bearable, each of them should do something different. So it was decided that he (Scott) would tell knock knock jokes for the first sixteen flights, Matt would sing tunes from musicals for the next sixteen flights and Henry would tell sad stories for the final sixteen.

Step by step they ascended for more than twenty-five tortuous minutes, through Scott's jokes, Matt's songs and finally Henry's sad sto-ries. As their room appeared before them at last, Henry reached into his pocket and sighed: 'Actu-ally, chaps, this is the saddest story of all. I left the room key at reception.'

An American couple spent their Christmas break driving across Mongolia. They turned on the vehicle's GPS for guidance. It said: 'Keep straight. Prepare to turn left on Tuesday morning.'

A man and his wife were competing in a couples Christmas golf tournament at a course in Florida. On the fifth hole the man hit his drive into deep rough and, after finding his ball, realized that a maintenance shed was directly in line with his intended shot to the green.

He was about to chip back onto the fairway – effectively wasting a stroke – when the husband in the opposing pair suggested: 'Wait a second. If we open the front and back doors of the shed, you may be able to hit a low two-iron and go right through the shed.'

The man thought it was worth a try. He lined up his shot, took a couple of practice swings and then fired a low two-iron towards the open doors. But he sliced it slightly and the ball smacked into the side of the shed, ricocheted at ninety degrees, hit his wife on the head and killed her instantly.

Naturally the man was devastated and refused to pick up his golf clubs for the next seven years. Eventually, however, a new friend talked him into taking up the game again, saying that it's what his late wife would have wanted. 'Just you and I, we'll play.'

His first game back was on the same course and, as fate would have it, his drive at the fifth hole landed in the same deep rough behind the same maintenance shed. His friend also suggested: 'If we open the doors of the shed, you might be able to hit a low shot straight through it.'

The idea brought back painful memories. The man stood in silence for a moment and then said: 'No, I'm sorry, I really don't want to do that. You see, I tried that shot seven years ago and took a double bogey!'

A man thought all of his Christmases had come at once when his sexy, recently divorced neighbour knocked on his door and asked him: 'Are you free tonight?'

'Sure,' he said, with a big grin on his face.

'Great!' she said. 'Would you look after my kids?'

When her husband came home unexpectedly on Christmas Eve, the wife hurriedly opened the bedroom window and told her lover to jump.

'What?! Are you crazy?' said the lover. 'This is the thirteenth floor!'

'Just jump!' said the wife. 'This is no time to be superstitious.'

A young couple wanted to get married on Christmas Day. When the vicar asked whether they would prefer a modern or a traditional service, they opted for the modern one.

On the morning of the wedding, a fierce snowstorm forced the groom to abandon the car and complete his journey to church on foot. The streets were so bad that he had to roll up his trousers in an attempt to keep them dry. As a result of the mishap, he arrived late at church and was immediately led up the aisle so that the ceremony could start.

The vicar looked at him and whispered: 'Pull down your trousers.'

The groom said nervously: 'Er, on second thoughts, Reverend, I've changed my mind. I think we'll go for the traditional service.'

A married couple went to a five-star hotel for a Christmas dinner dance. Towards the end of the evening a man in his late forties was really starting to strut his stuff on the dance floor. He was doing breakdancing, moonwalking and even throwing in a few back flips for good measure.

After watching this for a few minutes, the wife

turned to her husband and said: 'See that guy? Twenty-five years ago he proposed to me and I turned him down.'

The husband said: 'Looks like he's still celebrating!'

Travelling by train to visit his family in the north of England, a Londoner had to rely on the special Christmas Eve timetable, which meant fewer and slower trains, with the odd replacement bus service thrown in for good measure. Shortly after the train had set off from London, it slowed to a crawl through Hertfordshire until it finally came to a complete halt just south of Bedford. Seeing the guard walking alongside the track, the passenger leaned out of the window and inquired: 'What's happened?'

'There's a cow on the track,' replied the guard.

Ten minutes later, the train moved off and resumed its pitifully slow pace – but within five minutes it had stopped again.

The passenger then saw the same guard walking past outside, so he called out to the guard: 'What happened? Did we catch up with the cow again?'

A woman had agreed to look after her neighbour's male dog over Christmas, even though her own dog, a female, was on heat. She reasoned that the house was large enough for the two dogs to be kept apart but, just as she was drifting off to sleep, she heard a fearful howling sound coming from downstairs. Rushing down to investigate, she saw the two dogs locked together mating and unable to disengage.

She tried separating them but to no avail, so in a panic she phoned her vet, who made it clear that he was none too pleased to be disturbed at home at such a late hour over the holiday period. After she had explained the problem, he said tersely: 'Hang up the phone and then place it on the floor next to the dogs. I will then call you back and the noise of the phone ringing will make the male lose his erection and he will be able to withdraw.'

'Do you think that will work?' she asked.

The vet replied: 'Well, it just did for me.'

A couple decided to spend the Christmas break touring England. They took a chance by not booking any hotel rooms in advance but were sure they would still be able to find accommodation. However, when they arrived in a small market town, the only establishment with a room for the night was a distinctly modest pub named the George and Dragon.

Before they had a chance to speak, the landlady ran through the house rules. 'The room is £50 a night, cash only, payable in advance. We don't accept cheques or cards. No pets either. If you leave the building for any reason this evening, you must hand your room key to me and collect it upon your return. Do not take the key away from the premises. The doors will be locked at eleven thirty. If you are not back by then, you will be locked out for the night.

'In the morning, breakfast is seven thirty sharp in the dining room. If you are late, you will not get served. Checkout is by ten o'clock. Any later and you will incur additional charges to your bill. There will be a quick inspection of your room before you are allowed to leave to check for theft or damage. Any item falling into those categories will also be added to your bill. Is that clear? Any questions?'

The man said: 'Yes. Could I possibly speak to George?'

Two old men met up for their annual Christmas get-together. One said: 'I can't remember the last time I got lucky. It's been years since I had sex. How about you?'

His friend said: 'Well, I've still got what it takes to get a woman into the bedroom.'

'Oh yes. What's that?'

'A stairlift.'

A man had travelled abroad for Christmas. When he arrived at the rundown airport ready for his journey home, he was dismayed to see that his flight was delayed for five hours. So when it came to finally checking in, his mood was far from festive and not helped by the brusque attitude of the woman at the desk.

While his luggage was being weighed on the conveyor belt, he glanced up and saw a sprig of cheap, plastic mistletoe, presumably hanging there to represent the Christmas spirit. Venting his frustration at the check-in woman, he said: 'Even if I were single, I would not want to kiss you under the mistletoe in this ghastly airport.'

'Sir, look more closely where the mistletoe is located,' she said.

'Well, it's above the luggage scale, which is where you would have to step forward for a kiss.'

'That's not why it's there,' she said.

'OK,' he said. 'I give up. Why is it there?'

She cracked a smile and said: 'It's there so you can kiss your luggage goodbye.'

A teenage boy had become bored with spending the whole of Christmas Day at home with relatives. Instead he wanted to go to his friend's house, but his mother insisted that he had to stay and talk to his elderly aunts. In despair he turned to his father and said: 'Dad, when will I be old enough not to need Mum's permission to go out?'

'Don't ask me, son,' replied the father. 'Even I'm not yet old enough to go out without her permission!'

When a raging blizzard made it impossible for him to travel home, a company manager was resigned to spending a miserable Christmas alone in a hotel room. He lay on the bed, alternating between channel hopping on the TV and flicking through the pages of his only reading material, the Gideon Bible on the shelf.

Suddenly he had a flash of inspiration, put the Bible down and headed to reception, where the girl on the desk was an attractive redhead. As nobody else was around, he decided to strike up a conversation with her.

After the usual small talk about the weather and Christmas, he eventually asked her: 'What time do you finish?'

'Nine o'clock,' she replied.

'Would you like to come to my room for a Christmas drink after work?' he asked hopefully.

'Well, I'd like to, but I don't know whether I should.'

'It'll be okay,' he assured her. 'It says so in the Bible.'

'Okay then,' she said. 'I'll see you at nine.'

A few minutes after nine o'clock, she knocked on the door of his room. He let her in, invited her to sit on the bed and reached into the minibar for some drinks.

'How about a scotch and soda?' he suggested.

'I'd like to,' she said, 'but I'm not sure if I should.'

'It'll be fine,' he insisted. 'It says so in the Bible.'

'Well, in that case, all right.'

They had a couple of drinks, and then he suggested that they take off their clothes and get into bed for a cuddle.

'I'd like to,' she said, 'but I'm not sure it would be right.'

'Of course it would,' he said. 'It says so in the Bible.'

So they climbed into bed, and one thing led to another. Afterwards, as she got dressed, she asked him: 'Exactly whereabouts in the Bible does it say all this is okay?'

He reached for the Gideon Bible beside the bed and opened the front cover where someone had written: 'The redhead on reception is a sure thing.'

While on a Christmas safari in Kenya, a tourist was invited to a hunter's lodge, in which pride of place was taken by a huge, stuffed lion.

'Wow!' said the tourist. 'When did you bag that?'

'Five years ago,' said the hunter, 'while I was out in dense bush with my ex-wife.'

'And what's he stuffed with?' asked the tourist.

The hunter replied: 'My ex-wife.'

As they snuggled down together on Boxing Day night, alone at last, a wife asked her husband: 'How would you describe me?'

He said: 'ABCDEFGHIJK.'

'What does that mean?'

'Adorable, beautiful, cute, delightful, elegant, fashionable, glamorous and hot.'

'Oh, that's lovely,' she said. 'What about the IJK? What does that stand for?'

'I'm just kidding.'

Sharing a bottle of wine on Christmas evening, a seventy-year-old man began to feel quite mellow. Eventually he turned to his wife, looked her lovingly in the eyes and said: 'Darling, doesn't it make you sad when you see me chasing after younger women all the time?'

'Not really,' sniffed his wife. 'The dog is always chasing cars but there's no chance he'll ever manage to drive one!'

A husband heard his wife singing in the shower.
When she came out, he said: 'Darling, I wish
you'd sing Christmas carols.'
'That's nice of you,' she smiled. 'Is that because
you think they would suit my voice?'
'Not really,' he said, 'but it would mean I'd only
have to hear you sing once a year.'

On Christmas Eve, a couple were about to take their teenage daughter out for a celebratory dinner at a local restaurant. When the girl came downstairs from her bedroom she was wearing a short skirt and a tight top, prompting a grumpy lecture from her father about how unsuitable her outfit was for a smart restaurant. The girl's mother was more sympathetic and reminded him that when they were young she used to dress much the same way.

'That's true,' said the father, 'and if you remember, I had something to say about that, too.'

'Yes, you did,' said the mother. 'You asked me for my phone number.'

An Australian wedding reception was in full swing on Christmas Day. One of the guests, Kyle, had been delayed and was running late. When he finally reached the hotel, his mate, Stewie, was just leaving the party.

'I wouldn't go in there if I were you, mate,' warned Stewie. 'There's bound to be trouble.

They've run out of beer and the best man has just rooted the bride.'

So Kyle decided to turn back towards his car but just as he was about to leave, another guest rushed out of the hotel and shouted: 'Don't go, fellas. Everything's sorted. There's another keg on the way and the best man has apologized.'

A couple were driving into the heart of the countryside to spend Christmas at a smart hotel. Eager to avoid the Christmas rush on the motorways, the husband chose a route that would take them down narrow country lanes where he could really put his foot down on the gas. As he sped along one winding lane, his wife became increasingly nervous.

'Can't you slow down a bit when you're taking corners?' she complained. 'You're scaring the life out of me!'

'Just do what I do,' he replied. 'Shut your eyes.'

A theatre usher saw an old man crawling on his hands and knees during a Christmas pantomime production. She went over to him and said: 'Sir, you're disturbing several people around you. What's the problem?'

'I've lost my gum,' said the old man, continuing to search beneath the seats.

'Sir,' said the usher, 'if that's your only problem, let me offer you another stick of gum so that you can sit down and watch the show. A stick of gum is not worth all this commotion.'

'But you don't understand,' said the old man. 'My false teeth are in that gum!'

'I used to have a job as a pantomime horse,
but I quit while I was a head.'
STEWART FRANCIS

A man went into a library and asked the librarian for a book on pantomimes. The librarian said: 'It's behind you.'

*A pantomime horse walked into a bar and
asked for a beer. The bartender said:
'Would you like a pint?'
The pantomime horse said:
'No, two halves.'*

A couple who had been married for twenty-five years decided to spend Christmas at a country hotel. While they were lying in bed about to go to sleep, they heard a woman's voice from the adjoining room, saying: 'Oh, honey, you're so strong.'

The husband turned to his wife and said: 'Why don't you ever say that to me?'

'Because,' she replied, 'you're not strong anymore.'

A few minutes later, they heard the woman's voice again: 'Oh, honey, you're so romantic.'

The husband turned to his wife and said: 'Why don't you ever say that to me?'

'Because,' she replied, 'you're not romantic anymore.'

Five minutes later, they heard the woman groan: 'Oh, honey, that was an amazing orgasm. Thank you.'

The husband turned to his wife and said: 'Why don't you ever tell me when you have an amazing orgasm?'

'Because,' she replied, 'you're never around when I have them!'

A man in his early eighties decided to propose to his lady friend at Christmas. The following day he sent her an email: 'Dear Ethel, I must be getting so forgetful. I proposed to you last night, but have forgotten whether you said yes or no.'

Ethel emailed him back: 'Dear Alfred, it is good to hear from you. I know I said yes to someone last night, but I had forgotten exactly who it was.'

A woman rushed up the steps to the church,
late for the Christmas Day wedding.
An usher asked to see her invitation.
'I don't have one,' she said.
'Well, are you a friend of the groom?'
asked the usher.
'Certainly not!' she stormed.
'I'm the bride's mother!'

A couple spent Christmas at the Watergate Hotel in Washington, DC. The wife was worried in case the place was still bugged, so she asked her husband to conduct a thorough search of the room. He looked under the bed, behind the curtains, inside all the wardrobes and drawers and finally beneath the luxurious rug. And there, under the rug, he found a mysterious disc with four screws. Suspecting it to be a listening device, he removed the screws with his Swiss army knife and threw the disc out of the window.

When they checked out the following morning, the managed asked: 'How was your room? Was everything satisfactory and in good working order? How was the service? How was your room in terms of comfort? Was there anything you were unhappy about? On a scale of one to ten, how would you rate your stay at the Watergate?'

'Why are you asking so many questions?' said the husband.

'Well,' said the manager, 'I wanted to check that everything was OK because the people in the room below said the chandelier fell right on top of them.'

Spending their first Christmas together, a young couple were relaxing on Christmas night when he suddenly turned to her and asked: 'How many boyfriends did you have before me?'

She immediately fell silent for two or three minutes, prompting him to feel distinctly uneasy.

'Don't go all quiet on me,' he said eventually. 'Why didn't you answer my question?'

'Ssshhh!' she said. 'Don't interrupt me while I'm still counting.'

A man went to watch his favourite football team play a crucial Christmas game. The stadium was packed except for an empty seat next to him. When a latecomer arrived, he asked the man if the seat was taken.

'No, you can sit there,' said the man. 'My wife was supposed to be sitting in that seat, but she couldn't make it.'

'Where is she?'

'She died on Christmas Day. We'd been married for thirty-one years.'

'Oh, I'm so sorry to hear that. But shouldn't you give this seat to other family members?'

'No, they're all at the funeral.'

'There are two kinds of people in this world: those who count the days to 25 December and those who count the days to 26 December.'

LARENDA LYLES ROBERTS

Two old men, aged eighty-two and eighty-eight, met up for Christmas lunch. The eighty-eight-year-old had completed a five-mile run that morning. The younger man was impressed by his friend's stamina and asked him how he still came to have so much energy.

The eighty-eight-year-old said: 'I eat rye bread every day. It's a well-known fact that it keeps your energy levels high and that it will give you great stamina with the ladies.'

So at the first opportunity, the eighty-two-year-old stopped off at a bakery. As he was looking around the shop, the female sales clerk asked him if he needed any assistance.

'Do you have any rye bread?' he asked.

'Yes,' she said. 'There's a whole shelf of it. Would you like some?'

'Sure, I'll take five loaves.'

'Five loaves!' she exclaimed. 'By the time you get to the fifth loaf, it'll be hard.'

'I don't believe it!' he sighed. 'Everyone knows about this stuff except me!'

A couple argued bitterly over the Christmas period. It ended with the wife telling her sexist husband: 'I want more freedom.'
'No problem,' he said. 'I'll extend the kitchen.'

Father Murphy was feeling aggrieved that everyone except him seemed to be having fun at Christmas. So he turned to his fellow priest, Father O'Riordan, and said: 'I'm sick of all this good behaviour and clean living. Just for once, why don't we have a good old sinful night out? We could drink as much as we can take, go with loose women and do whatever we please. What do you say?'

'Are you crazy?' said Father O'Riordan. 'This is a small town. Everyone knows who we are. We only have to glance at a pretty girl in the street and the bishop gets to hear about it!'

'I don't mean we should go wild here,' explained Father Murphy. 'I agree that we're too well known. But if we dressed in ordinary clothes, we could take the train to the city and have a fine time – and nobody would be any the wiser.'

After much persuasion, Father O'Riordan eventually agreed to the plan. They caught the train to the city that evening and partied until dawn. They arrived back home very much the worse for wear and that was when the enormity of what they had done began to register with him.

'Oh my God!' he said, wiping the sweat from his brow. 'We're going to have to confess to our sins.'

'Don't worry,' said Father Murphy. 'I've already thought about this. You get changed and go into the confessional. I'll tell you all about my misdemeanours and you can absolve me. Then I'll do the same for you.'

So, half an hour later, Father Murphy went to the church and entered the confessional. 'Father, forgive me for I have sinned. I went out with a friend last night to celebrate Christmas. I got drunk, slept with two women, danced to wicked music and used profane language.'

On the other side of the curtain, Father O'Riordan replied: 'God is patient and forgiving and so am I. Do five Our Fathers, five Hail Marys and your sins will be forgiven.'

A few minutes later, their positions were reversed and Father O'Riordan confessed to everything that had taken place in the city.

'This is outrageous,' boomed Father Murphy. 'What kind of priest are you? Do five hundred Our Fathers, five hundred Hail Marys, donate all your income for the next six months to the church, and crawl around the church on your knees twenty times, begging for God's forgiveness as you do so. Then come back to me and maybe – only maybe – I'll consider absolution.'

'What do you mean?!' exclaimed Father O'Riordan in horror. 'What happened to our agreement?'

'Listen,' replied Father Murphy. 'What I do with my time off is one thing, but I take my job very seriously.'

After three days of having to entertain and cook over Christmas, a woman was ready to let her hair down. So when the last of her guests had departed, she said to her husband: 'Let's go out and have some fun tonight.'

'Great idea,' he said, 'but if you get home before I do, leave the hallway light on.'

THANK GOODNESS THAT'S OVER FOR ANOTHER YEAR

A few days after Christmas, a mother was working in the kitchen listening to her young son playing with his new train set in the lounge. She heard the train stop and her son say: 'All of you sons of bitches who want to get off, get the hell off now because this is the last stop. And all of you sons of bitches who are getting on, get your asses in the train, because we're leaving now.'

The mother was horrified to hear her son use such language and sent him to his room for two hours. 'After that,' she said, 'you may play with your train, but only if you use nice language.'

Two hours later, the son emerged from his bedroom and resumed playing with his toy train. Soon the train stopped and the mother heard him say: 'All passengers who are disembarking from the train, please remember to take all of your belongings with you. We thank you for riding with us today and hope your journey was a pleasant one. We hope you will travel again with us soon.

'For those of you just boarding, we ask you to stow all of your hand luggage in the overhead racks. Remember there is no smoking on this train and please have your tickets ready for inspection. We hope you will have a pleasant and relaxing journey with us today.'

As the mother began to smile, the son added: 'For those of you who are pissed off about the two-hour delay, please see the bitch in the kitchen.'

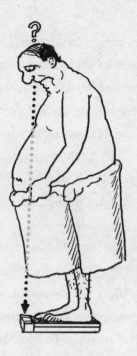

Ten days after Christmas, a man was standing on the bathroom scales, desperately holding his stomach in.

Thinking he was trying to reduce his weight, his wife remarked: 'I don't think that will help.'

'It does,' he said. 'It's the only way I can read the numbers!'

'I come from a very traditional family. When I was seven, my Uncle Terry hanged himself on Christmas Eve. My family didn't take his body down until 6 January.'
NICK DOODY

A man with a bald head and a wooden leg was invited to a New Year's fancy dress party. Unsure of what costume to wear to hide his head and leg, he wrote to a fancy dress company for suggestions. A few days later he received a parcel with a note that read: 'Please find enclosed a pirate's costume. The spotted handkerchief will cover your bald head and, with your wooden leg, you will make a great pirate.'

The man was angry because the outfit emphasized his wooden leg, so he wrote a letter of complaint to the company. A week later he received another parcel with a note that read: 'Sorry about the pirate's costume, and please find enclosed a monk's habit. The long robe will cover your wooden leg and with your bald head, you will really look the part.'

The man was furious because this outfit emphasized his bald head, so he wrote another letter of complaint to the company. The next day he received a parcel with a note that read: 'Please find enclosed a jar of caramel. Pour the caramel over your bald head, stick your wooden leg up your ass and go as a toffee apple!'

'It goes Christmas, New Year's Eve and Valentine's Day. Is that fair to anyone who's alone? If you didn't get around to killing yourself on Christmas or New Year's, boom, there's Valentine's Day for you. There should be a holiday after Valentine's Day called "Are You Still Here?"'
LAURA KIGHTLINGER

A man had received a chainsaw as a Christmas present. It was guaranteed to cut through six trees in an hour, but two days later he took it back to the store and complained: 'This chainsaw is useless! It took me all day to cut down one tree.'

To find out what the problem might be, the sales assistant took the chainsaw and started it up.

The man looked startled and said: 'What's that noise?'

When his wife went missing the day after Boxing Day, her husband searched everywhere for her. As well as reporting her disappearance to the police, he contacted all her friends and family in a bid to trace her. Then two days after she had vanished, he returned home to find her standing in the bathroom.

'Where have you been? I've been worried sick about you!'

She said: 'Four masked men kidnapped me, tied me up and had wild sex with me for a week.'

'But it's only been two days,' said the husband. 'What do you mean, a week?'

She replied: 'I'm only here to collect my toothbrush.'

A man went to the doctor's complaining that he had been in discomfort since Christmas. 'It's this terrible blinking and twitching in my right eye. I just can't control it. Please help me, Doc.'

The doctor examined him thoroughly and said: 'Actually, it's not as bad as you think.'

'You don't understand,' said the man. 'Every time I go to the pharmacy to get some painkillers, they give me condoms!'

On 6 January, a couple decided that next year's Christmas was going to be their best ever. They were going to pull out all the stops, no expense spared. To pay for it, they set up a Christmas fund and came up with the idea that each time they had sex they would put £20 into a piggy bank.

After ten months of this, they reckoned there was probably more than enough money in the piggy bank to pay for their dream Christmas, so they opened it. The husband was puzzled by what he found. 'That's odd,' he said. 'Each time we had sex, I put £20 in. But look at all these £50 notes.'

The wife replied: 'That's your trouble – you think everybody is as stingy as you.'

Two next-door neighbours met on the street while they were washing their cars.

'How was your Christmas?' asked one.

'Not bad,' said the other. 'We didn't do much, just stayed in most of the time. How about you?'

'Well, we were planning to go and see a show in town last night, but when my wife was getting ready and asked me to pass a lipstick to her I accidentally handed her a glue stick instead.'

'Oh dear. How did she react?'

'Let's just say she still isn't talking to me.'

When the company returned to work on 27 December, the boss asked one of his employees: 'Do you believe in life after death?'

'I'm not sure, sir,' he replied. 'Why do you ask?'

'Because,' said the boss, 'after you asked to leave work early on Christmas Eve so that you could attend your grandmother's funeral, she dropped by to see you!'

An accountant was walking along the street just before Christmas when he was accosted by a beggar.

'Could you part with a couple of pounds, sir?' said the beggar. 'I haven't eaten for three days.'

'I see,' said the accountant. 'And how does this compare to the same period last year?'

A wife decided to have a New Year clearout. She was bagging up some old clothes before taking them to the charity shop when she reached into the pocket of one of her husband's old suits and discovered a shoe repairer's ticket. Later, she showed the ticket to her husband.

'This ticket must be twenty years old,' he said. 'I must have forgotten to collect those shoes. That shop is still there, so I'll take the ticket in and see whether they've still got them.'

He went back to the shoe shop with the ticket. The sales assistant glanced at it and said: 'They'll be ready Thursday.'

At the start of the New Year, a man thought
about the evils of drinking. So he decided to
make that his New Year's resolution
– to give up thinking.

An elderly couple had been married for forty-seven years. Much to the wife's annoyance, every morning as soon as he woke up her husband would release a seismic fart in bed. 'One of these days you'll fart your guts out!' she told him.

One year on the day after Christmas she finally decided to take her revenge. Creeping out of bed early, she fetched the leftover turkey giblets from Christmas dinner and gently placed them in the bed next to her sleeping husband's butt.

Fifteen minutes later while she was downstairs making breakfast, she heard his usual morning fart reverberate through the floorboards followed by an equally loud scream. Not long afterwards her husband appeared in the kitchen, ashen-faced.

'You were right,' he told her. 'I did fart my guts out but, by the grace of God and these two fingers, I managed to push 'em back in!'

What's the biggest problem with
jogging on New Year's Eve?

~

The ice falls out of
your drink.

A drunk staggered into a bar and shouted out:
'Happy New Year everybody!'

'What are you talking about?' said the barman.
'It's the middle of June!'

'Oh my God!' exclaimed the drunk. 'My wife is
going to kill me. I've never been so late in my life!'

If you were born in September, you can safely
assume your parents celebrated New Year
with a bang.

A married couple were invited to a New Year's fancy dress party. They were looking forward to it but at the last minute the wife cried off with a headache. Not wanting to spoil the evening for her husband, she insisted he went on his own. So he set off for the party in his full Batman costume.

After lying on the bed for an hour, the wife started to feel better and decided that she was well enough to go to the party after all. When she arrived, the party was in full swing. She quickly spotted Batman but chose to keep her presence a secret from her husband, something she was able to do since he had no idea what her costume was. Instead she preferred to observe him from a distance, to see how he behaved when she wasn't around.

She watched from the other side of the room as he flirted, kissed and danced with a succession of other women before deciding that it was time to make a move on him herself, still without revealing her identity.

Disguising her voice, she sidled up to him and said: 'Fancy a breath of fresh air?'

'Sure,' he replied. 'I know the perfect place.'

And with that, he led her into the car park,

where they had sex over the bonnet of a car.

Both returned to the party, but shortly before midnight she slipped home alone, removed her costume and went to bed. Waiting for her husband to come home, she wondered how he would try and explain his behaviour at the party.

He finally arrived home just after 1.30 am.

'How was it?' she asked.

'Oh, you know I never have a good time when you're not there, darling.'

'Did you dance?'

'No, not one dance. In fact, when I got there, I met a few pals and we went to the den and played poker all evening.'

'Oh, yeah?' said the wife.

'But I tell you,' he continued, 'the guy I loaned my Batman costume to sure got lucky!'

Two men were sitting in the pub on New Year's Day discussing New Year's resolutions. One said: 'I don't believe in them. They're just a waste of time, and nobody keeps to them for more than a day anyway.'

'I did actually think about making one this year,' said the other, sipping his beer. 'I planned to quit drinking for the New Year.'

'So what happened?'

'I remembered that nobody likes a quitter.'

A husband looked despairingly at the bedroom mirror to see all the weight he had put on over Christmas. His stomach appeared really flabby. Just then his wife walked in.

'It's not a pretty sight, is it?' he admitted. 'I'm getting really fat. I could do with a compliment.'

She said: 'Your eyesight's good.'

As a New Year's gift for his wife, a man paid for her and three friends to spend two days at a health farm. When she returned and after she had unpacked all her clothes, she was startled to find a pair of panties that didn't belong to her crumpled up in the laundry room.

Snatching them up, she immediately marched into the lounge to confront her husband.

He protested his innocence, saying: 'I have no idea where they came from. I don't do the laundry – the maid does.'

The wife calmed down and said: 'Oh, OK, I'll give you the benefit of the doubt. Maybe the maid was doing her laundry here and these panties belong to her.'

'I doubt it,' said the husband. 'She never wears any.'

An iPhone and a firework were arrested on New Year's Eve. One was charged and the other was let off.

A man stood at the dock in court on trial for murder. The judge said: 'On 26 December last year you are charged with bludgeoning your wife to death with a hammer. How do you plead?'

'Guilty,' replied the defendant.

Hearing this, a man in the public gallery stood

up and yelled: 'You dirty stinking rat!'

The judge ordered the man to sit down and to refrain from passing further comment. The judge then continued addressing the defendant: 'And on 13 January this year you are charged with bludgeoning your brother-in-law to death with a hammer. How do you plead?'

'Guilty,' replied the defendant.

At this, the same man in the public gallery got to his feet and screamed: 'You dirty, filthy, stinking bastard!'

'Order! Order!' cried the judge. He then summoned the man to the bench and warned him: 'I have already told you to be quiet, but if you persist in interrupting these proceedings I shall charge you with contempt of court. I appreciate that feelings are running high in this case, but what connection exactly do you have with the defendant?'

'He's my next-door neighbour, Your Honour,' said the man.

'Well, as I say,' the judge said sternly, 'I can understand your feelings given that you probably knew both of the deceased, but you must behave in court.'

'No, Your Honour, you don't understand,' said the man. 'Twice I asked him if I could borrow a hammer, and both times he told me he didn't have one!'

'Women get a little more excited about New Year's Eve than men do. It's like an excuse: you drink too much, you make a lot of promises you're not going to keep; the next morning as soon as you wake up you start breaking them. For men, we just call that a date.'
JAY LENO

On New Year's Eve, a woman stood up in her local pub and announced to the assembled gathering that at the stroke of midnight she wanted every husband to stand next to the person who made his life worth living. As the clock struck midnight, the bartender was almost crushed to death.

In the middle of January, a man went to his local police station to report that his wife had gone missing.

'When did you last see her?' asked the duty sergeant.

'On Christmas Day,' replied the man.

'Why has it taken you almost a month to report her missing?'

'Well, this week I've run out of clean clothes to wear.'

Concerned that she had put on weight over Christmas, a fifty-year-old woman went for a health check early in the New Year. When she arrived back home, she was grinning from ear to ear.

'What are you looking so pleased about?' asked her husband.

She said: 'The doctor told me that for a fifty-year-old woman, I have the face and skin of a thirty-year-old.'

'What did he say about your fifty-year-old ass?'

'Your name never came up in the conversation!'

A man told a friend: 'Some people in our street are having a joint Burns Night and Chinese New Year party this weekend.'

'OK. That's an interesting combination,' said the friend.

'Yes, they're calling it Chinese Burns Night. I wasn't going to go but they twisted my arm.'

A woman asked her husband how his New Year's weight loss regime was going.

'I've lost 20lbs,' he told her proudly.

'Wow! That's great,' she said, hesitantly. 'I don't mean to sound unkind, but it doesn't look as if you have lost that much weight. Are you sure?'

'Absolutely,' he replied. 'I've lost the same 5lbs four times now.'

When the surgery reopened after Christmas, a man went to see his doctor.

'Did you sleep by an open window as I suggested?' asked the doctor.

'Yes, I did,' said the man.

'And have you lost your bronchitis?'

'No. So far all I've lost is my laptop and my phone!'

Following a fraught, traumatic Christmas punctu-ated by rows with her overweight, slovenly hus-band, a woman went into a pharmacy and asked for some arsenic.

'What do you need arsenic for?' asked the pharmacist.

She said: 'I want to kill my husband.'

'I'm sorry,' said the pharmacist, 'but I can't sell you arsenic so that you can kill your husband.'

The woman then reached into her handbag, pulled out a photo of her husband and showed it to the pharmacist.

'Oh,' he said, 'you didn't tell me you had a prescription.'

Did you hear about the man whose
New Year's resolution
was to read more?

~

So he pressed the 'subtitles'
button on his TV remote.

To start the New Year, a father decided to give his three-year-old son his first pocket money. 'I'll give you two pence a week, son, so you save it up and put it in this yellow box. Then when you've got five, I'll swap them for a ten pence coin and you can put that in this blue box. Then when you've got five of those, I'll swap them for a fifty pence coin and you can put that in this red box.'

It was twelve years before the boy discovered that the red box was the gas meter.

Two men were talking about their healthy New Year's resolutions. One said: 'Mine is to help all my friends gain 10lbs so that I look slimmer.'

The other said: 'Mine is to finally go to the gym ... and cancel that membership I've been wasting my money on every month since last January.'

*'Every New Year's I celebrate making it
through another holiday season
without killing my relatives.'*
MELANIE WHITE

Having had way too much to drink on New Year's Eve, a man left his car at the pub and set off on the walk home. As he was swaying along, he was stopped by a police officer.

'What are you doing out at five o'clock in the morning?' asked the officer.

'I'm on my way to a lecture,' answered the man with slurred speech.

'Who on earth is going to give a lecture at this hour?' asked the officer, incredulously.

The man looked him in the eye as best as he could and replied: 'My wife.'

*An optimist stays up until midnight
to see the New Year in. A pessimist
stays up to make sure the
old year leaves.*

David worked for the Post Office where it was his job to process all the mail that had illegible addresses. A week or so before Christmas, a letter landed on his desk. It had shaky handwriting and was simply addressed to 'God'. With no other clues on the envelope, David decided to open it and read the letter inside. It went:

'Dear God, I am a ninety-two-year-old widow living on the state pension. Yesterday someone stole my purse. It had £100 in it, which was all the money I had in the world. My next pension payment is not due until after Christmas, but I have invited two of my friends over for Christmas lunch. Without that money, I cannot buy any food. I have no family to turn to, so you are my only hope. Please God, can you help me?'

David was so touched by the letter that he pinned it on the notice board at the sorting office. His colleagues were equally moved, and all the mail workers clubbed together and managed to raise £95 to send to the old lady. An envelope containing the cash was duly returned to her address, and the Post Office staff were able to enjoy their Christmas safe in the knowledge that they had performed a noble, charitable deed.

When they were back at work in the first week of January, another letter simply addressed to 'God' ended up in the sorting office. Everyone gathered round while David opened it and read the contents aloud. It went:

'Dear God, thank you so much for your kind gesture. Because of your generosity, I was able to provide a lovely Christmas lunch for my friends. We had a wonderful day together, and I told them about your gift. Even Father Derek, our parish priest, was overcome with joy. By the way, there was £5 missing. I think it must have been those thieving BASTARDS at the Post Office.'